THE SPIRIT OF THE PSALMS

by Noël Quesson
Translated and edited by Marie-France Curtin

Paulist Press
New York/Mahwah, N.J.

Originally published as *50 Psaumes pour tous les jours* by Droguet & Ardant, Limoges, France. Copyright © 1978 by Droguet–Ardant. English translation © 1990 by The Missionary Society of St. Paul the Apostle in the State of New York.

Library of Congress Cataloging-in-Publication Data

Quesson, Noël.
    [50 psaumes pour tous les jours. English]
    The spirit of the Psalms: a handbook for reading and praying the Psalms with Israel, with Jesus, and with the present moment/by Noël Quesson; translated by Marie-France Curtin.
    p. cm.
    Translation of: 50 psaumes pour tous les jours.
    ISBN 0-8091-3199-4
    1. Bible. O.T. Psalms—Devotional literature. 2. Bible. O.T. Psalms—Criticism, interpretation, etc. I. Title.
BS1430.4.Q8413   1990   90-46959
223'.206—dc20   CIP

Published by Paulist Press
997 Macarthur Boulevard
Mahwah, New Jersey 07430

Printed and bound in the
United States of America

CONTENTS

Introduction 1

Psalms

INTRODUCTION

In the days of old, only those Christians who took part in Sunday Vespers would sing a few psalms—five to be exact, which were repeated practically every Sunday, with the exception of feast days. Fortunately, the liturgical reform of Vatican II gave us back the book of Psalms in its entirety. Nowadays, a different psalm is offered to all Christians every Sunday in the very heart of the mass. We now have at our disposal eighty psalms which were practically unknown to most of the faithful, but which are now becoming a part of our prayer life. But this new wealth of prayers does not always fit with our daily life. One of my friends said to me recently: "I can't pray with the psalms!"

WHY THE PSALMS ARE SO DIFFICULT

The psalms are admittedly strange prayers. They were born a little over twenty centuries ago, in a period of history quite different from our own. They were composed by a very special people, Israel, who added to them its own history (Moses, David), its own geography (Zion, Jerusalem, Lebanon, Moab), and all of its political or religious institutions (the kings, the Temple, the Jewish holidays).

André Chouraqui, a Jew by birth, comments: "We were born with this book in our very guts." This is so true. . . . It is therefore necessary for us who are not Jews to be guided through these poems.

THE IRREPLACEABLE VALUE OF THE PSALMS

The book of Psalms has always been, and remains an important book of prayer for the church. No book has been more often translated, quoted, and annotated.

Why is this book one of the best schools of prayer? It is an "inspired prayer," a prayer whose main author is God: it is part

1

of the Bible, which is the word of God. It is, nevertheless, a book written by human authors who composed it with every fiber of their human selves. These poems have been molded with flesh and blood, they are "mirrors of our rebellions and our infidelities, of our agonies and our resurrections" (A. Chouraqui).

THE BOOK OF SONGS SUNG BY JESUS

The psalms are the songs Jesus sang in the synagogue at Nazareth. We know which words Jesus was singing or reciting as he "went up" to Jerusalem on a pilgrimage; we know which psalms he sang in the evening of Holy Thursday, just before his agony and death.

We can be practically certain that Jesus knew the 150 psalms by heart. In his time, there were no fads, no passing fashions. From the day of his birth to the day of his death, on every single Sabbath, a Jew would hear the same texts which he could easily memorize.

We can then imagine the strong impact the psalms must have had on the whole thought and prayer of Jesus. We have explicit proof of this in the passage from Luke (24:44–46) when our Lord appears to his apostles after the resurrection and tells them: "This is what I meant when I said, while I was still with you, that everything written about me in the Law of Moses, in the Prophets and in the Psalms, was destined to be fulfilled." He then opened their minds to understand the scriptures, and he said to them: "So it is written that the Christ would suffer and on the third day rise from the dead."

The purpose of this book is to offer suggestions on how to open our minds to an understanding of the psalms, since many of them need to be explained in order for us to grasp all their depth.

There are three possible readings which help us to comprehend the psalms fully, each of which throws light upon the others.

OUR READING METHOD

1. A First Reading: With Israel
A minimum of exegetical knowledge is necessary to uncover the literal meaning, which is the first step. Through literary and

historical analysis, we can discover the situations which gave birth to these poems. We must ask ourselves what the psalms meant for the Jews themselves.

2. A Second Reading: With Jesus

However beautiful these sacred texts may be from a literary point of view, the church of today does not offer them to us to perpetuate a culture which is no longer ours (and the semitisms we shall have to explain are a proof of this). The goal of the church is to sing the mysteries of Christ, and we shall see that the gospel of Jesus is indeed filled with the thoughts of the psalms. The church is therefore not doing anything artificial by offering them to us today, since the psalms were the prayers of Jesus. There are more than twenty explicit quotes from the book of Psalms on the very lips of our Lord.

This rereading—with Jesus—of texts written before the time of Jesus enables us, not to expurgate them, but to read them in a new way.

3. A Third Reading: With Our Time

We are indeed people of the twentieth century, and God does not ask us to go backwards. Starting with the two preceding studies, our purpose is therefore to pray each psalm in the context of our own life, in our own time frame, with the thought-processes of today, and with the church of our time. By repeating these ancient prayers, the church does not want to preserve museum pieces; she is right in the here-and-now of the world.

As a result, each individual can say: No one can replace me in applying these psalms concretely to my daily life, and I must return to these ancient words with my personal situation, my temperament, my worries, my joys and my sorrows, my responsibilities and my plans for the future.

ILLUSTRATIONS, IMAGES

As you become familiar with the psalter, you will be amazed to see how very concrete and full of imagery its language is. Hebrew is not an abstract language, and this is a boon for the poetic quality of the book. Many of the images are universal, and correspond to the simplest form of culture, to that shared by all peoples: the flower that blooms at dawn and wilts at dusk, the water that submerges and fertilizes, the verdant tree that yields its fruit, the fortress that protects the city, the storm that terrifies, the star-studded sky that fills one with wonder.

In the liturgy of the mass, the psalm is always carefully chosen to accompany the first reading and the gospel. It is often the psalm that sets the tone for a particular Sunday.

If we are faithful to the message of the psalms, we are not likely to fall into the trap of private piety. We are sure, rather, to go out into the world, and fight for the kingdom of God. Whoever drinks regularly from that "torrent" cannot but participate in the building of a new world. Our ancestors expressed it well when they said *Ora et labora*. This can still be our motto today: "WORSHIP AND WORK."

Noël Quesson

PSALM 1

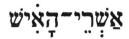

THE WAY OF THE VIRTUOUS

1 Happy indeed is the man
   who follows not the counsel of the wicked;
   nor lingers in the way of sinners
   nor sits in the company of scorners,
2 but whose delight is the law of the Lord
   and who ponders his law day and night.

3 He is like the tree that is planted
   beside the flowing waters,
   that yields its fruit in due season
   and whose leaves shall never fade;
   and all that he does shall prosper.
4 Not so are the wicked, not so!

   For they like winnowed chaff
   shall be driven away by the wind.
5 When the wicked are judged they shall not stand,
   nor find room among those who are just;
6 for the Lord guards the way of the just
   but the way of the wicked leads to doom.

■

HAPPINESS IS THE WAY OF THE VIRTUOUS
   —in a negative way: we must stay away from the contagion
     of evil
   —in a positive way: we must meditate on the word of God
   This leads to vitality, fecundity
   Like a verdant tree

NOTHINGNESS IS THE WAY OF THE WICKED
    Like a chaff of wheat
    In the eschatological day of the Lord
    In the day of truth about everything

CONCLUSION
    The virtuous are beloved by God
    The wicked are nothingness

■

1. A FIRST READING: WITH ISRAEL

This psalm was not placed in the beginning of the psalter by chance. The first word of the psalm begins with *Aleph,* the first letter of the Hebrew alphabet, and the last word of the psalm begins with *Tav,* which is the last letter of the alphabet. The fourth evangelist uses the same literary device when he says that Jesus Christ is the Alpha and the Omega, the Beginning and the End. This psalm truly sums up the entire Law and gives us, in just a few words, everything we need to know, from A to Z.

Two roads are open to every human being:

—one road leads to the happiness symbolized by the verdant tree;

—the other road leads to the nothingness symbolized by the chaff being blown away by the wind.

The author did not create a perfect, mechanical symmetry which would have placed too much emphasis on evil. Therefore, he uses ten lines of the text to describe in detail the rooted, steadfast existence of the virtuous and devotes only five lines to the ephemeral, meaningless existence of the wicked.

This psalm is part of the Ritual of the Covenant and may have been sung at the Festival of the Tents, during which the Covenant was renewed. It is a prophetic announcement of the blessings which are bestowed upon those who are faithful to the Covenant and the curses which plague those who are unfaithful to it (see Jeremiah 17:5–8 for a similar text).

Psalm 1, in its brevity, is truly the prelude to the whole psalter. It also sums up human life. Here, we have at play the mighty conflict between good and evil which will result in the victory of good. The psalmist expresses his hope and his certitude that God's plan will succeed. Do we have this same optimism for the dynamics of the future? The messianic era which Israel is waiting for *is* happiness and success.

2. A SECOND READING: WITH JESUS

It is not by chance that the first word of the Good News of the kingdom announced by Jesus is the same as here: Happy, *Asherei.* Jesus' thought is summed up in the Beatitudes, which in

Luke's version (6:20–26) are accompanied by curses, just as in this psalm.

Jesus often used the image of the tree which produces good fruit (Mt 7:17–20), and grows until it shelters the birds of the air (Mt 13:32). He compared himself to a vine that yields its fruit in due season (Jn 15:1).

Let us take note of some very powerful metaphors: the stream of living water which allows the tree to remain verdant and which, Jesus tells us, is the Holy Spirit (Jn 4:14, 7:38). In the sacrament of baptism, water is also the symbol of renewed life (Jn 3:5). Likewise—although it is certain that the psalmist did not think about the cross when he was talking about a tree which yields its fruit—we can meditate—in truth—on these comparisons which are much more than mere symbols: In the Garden of Eden, God had also planted a Tree of Life (Gn 2:9; Rv 2:7).

3. A THIRD READING: WITH OUR TIME

In our modern world, we may be tempted to believe this psalm is unrealistic and too beautiful to be true. We do, after all, witness the failure of the virtuous and the success of the wicked! Job knew this already, and it has been the scandal of all times. Jesus himself, the most virtuous of all men, ended his life on the withered tree of the cross, in what appeared to be the most dismal of failures. But let us listen to the wise words of the psalmist who, speaking from experience, assures us that everything the virtuous attempt prospers. We must listen carefully to this paradoxical statement and understand it in terms of faith and not in terms of immediate material success.

The ideas of "nothingness" and "absurdity" are very modern. Many contemporary writers justify, without knowing it, the wise thought of the psalmist by their disillusioned reflections; it is very obvious that human beings are nothing without God.

In contrast to these desperate ideas, how precious is the optimistic hope of the psalmist. For, if our human existence is meaningless without God, with God it becomes a fantastic life energy suggested by the image of the tree. Yes, something *is* maturing, and Jesus reminded us of this with emphasis. Our earth *will* yield its fruit. Creation is a formidable evolutionary power which proceeds toward success, toward the successful completion of the work which God started and will accomplish to its fullest. How far we are from a narrow understanding of the term "success" which earlier made us doubt the realism of this psalm! How very far we are from what has been termed "temporal revenge." The happiness we are talking about here is the happiness of the poor, of the "anawim." Blessed are the poor! They are not promised money! They are promised happiness and a successful life in God.

You also can enjoy this happiness and this success *today*. Refuse the contagion of evil! Do not follow the way of the wicked! Take your Good News and meditate on it day and night! To live is to choose, so let us choose God! Let this be your daily, heartfelt meditation! This is where you will find happiness—true happiness—which nothing can destroy.

PSALM 8

יְהוָה אֲדֹנֵינוּ מָה־אַדִּיר שִׁמְךָ

HOW GREAT IS YOUR NAME

2   How great is your name, O Lord our God,
    through all the earth!

    Your majesty is praised above the heavens;
3   on the lips of children and of babes
    you have found praise to foil your enemy,
    to silence the foe and the rebel.

4   When I see the heavens, the work of your hands,
    the moon and the stars which you arranged,
5   what is man that you should keep him in mind,
    mortal man that you care for him?

6   Yet you have made him little less than a god;
    with glory and honor you crowned him,
7   gave him power over the works of your hand,
    put all things under his feet.

8   All of them, sheep and cattle,
    yes, even the savage beasts,
9   birds of the air, and fish
    that make their way through the waters.

10 How great is your name, O Lord our God,
    through all the earth!

■

HYMN TO THE MAJESTY OF GOD
The "heavens" (image of the majesty of God) were obviously not created by human hands!

In contrast, there is "man," insignificant, ephemeral, fragile (man = "the mortal one," the son of Adamah, "the one
made out of clay").

HYMN TO THE DIGNITY OF MAN
a sort of "king":

crown glory, honor . . .
lord and master of everything . . .
   —on earth
   —in the air
   —and on the oceans . . .

But all the dignity of man has been given to him by God,
and in the end sings his glory.

■

A FIRST READING: WITH ISRAEL

This hymn to the lordship of Yahweh must have been sung at night, under a star-studded sky, during one of these cloudless, translucent Oriental nights.

This psalm expresses in song and prayer the basic teaching, the elementary catechesis of the Jewish faith, found in the book of Genesis: God created the entire universe, God created man and woman and entrusted the world to them: "Let us make man in our own image, in the likeness of ourselves. . . . Fill the earth and subdue it . . . I give you all . . ." (Gn 1).

A remarkable characteristic of this psalm of praise to the greatness of *God* is that it becomes in the end—and at length—a psalm of praise to the greatness of humanity. But nevertheless, God is always in the forefront.

Consider the personal pronouns and possessive adjectives used in the psalm: *your* name, *your* majesty, *you* set, *your* fingers, *you* created, *you* spare a thought for them, *you* care for him, *your* hands, etc. Paradoxically, we can see that in a poem in which men and women are so highly exalted, *God* is the actual subject of nearly every verb!

A SECOND READING: WITH JESUS

Jesus explicitly quoted this psalm when he came to the defense of the simple people who were acclaiming him on Palm Sunday: "Do you hear what they are saying?" they said to him." Jesus answered, "Yes. Have you never read this: 'By the mouths of children, babes in arms, you have made sure of praise'?" (Mt 21:16).

Thus, for Jesus, the true greatness of humanity is the greatness of these "children" who accept everything with simplicity. Elsewhere, Jesus does stress the necessity for humility: "I bless you, Father . . . for hiding these things from the learned and the clever and revealing them to little children" (Lk 10:21).

Saint Paul quotes this psalm three more times (Heb 2:6–10; Ep 1:22; I Co 15:25–27). "You put all things under his feet." Every time Paul quotes this passage, he wants to stress the miracle of Christ's resurrection, and his total victory over death.

According to Fr. Martelet: "God's promise to set all things under our feet is preposterous dupery if man remains defeated by death . . . for then, man is the one who is lying on the ground, at the feet of all living creatures." But the Second Adam fulfills precisely—and to the fullest—the promise made to the first Adam. Jesus *is* the man to whom God gave dominion over everything. When Pilate said: "Here is the *man*," he did not realize how profoundly true his statement was. Indeed, what answer can one give to the person who poses the fundamental questions: "What is man? What is the meaning of his frailty compared to astral infinity?" There is only one possible answer: Man is the "human condition" which the Son of God chose to take upon himself." The word became flesh . . . God became man!" Therefore we should not be surprised that this psalm—an inspired song—sings the "glory of man" while singing the "glory of God."

A THIRD READING: WITH OUR TIME

1. *Wonder*—The more science tells us about the marvels of the universe, the more we are able to sing this psalm with conviction. "When I see the heavens, the work of your hands." We should be filled with awe knowing that the universe is immense, that the cosmos can only be measured in millions of light-years.

2. *Childhood*—This is one of the main themes of contemporary literature: the freshness and the truth of the many "whys" of our children: "Daddy, why does the sun give us light?"—"Because it is made out of fire."—"Why is it made out of fire?" We must look at the world with the wonder of a child.

3. *The Stars and the Sky*—They are magnificent, aren't they? Let their beauty overwhelm you on a beautiful summer night, as you lie in a meadow. Human beings could not possibly have created all of this beauty! Children are able to grasp what conceited adults will never be able to understand: the firmament is that stronghold which God's adversary, in his infinite weakness, will never be able to conquer! God does not need to defend himself. No enemy shall ever reach him! The harmonious laws that govern the cosmos and the stellar infinity reduce to silence the presumptuous fools who think they can recreate

the universe. Our ancestors did possess the truth when they claimed to "hear the celestial bodies sing" (Job 38:7-11). Please do listen to the song of the stars!

4. *Technology: Man Over Nature*—There is no contradiction in terms. "You put all things under his feet." One day, astronauts set foot on the moon. What a symbolic manifestation of the greatness of humankind who progressively becomes ruler of the universe! Yet, no poet from space, no press communiqué, no official report from NASA dared say about man what the people of God have been saying for centuries in psalm 8: "You have made him little less than a god; with glory and honor you crowned him, gave him power over the works of your hand . . ."

In the days of the psalmist, any voyager who boarded a ship, "making his way through the waters," had dominion over the ocean, according to God's design. In our day, the pilot who takes off in his jet and lands a few hours later in another continent also carries out one of God's designs, often without even knowing it.

5. *What Is Man?*—Pascal's question is still extraordinarily modern. Faced with the immensity of the universe, man does feel insignificant: "The eternal silence of these infinite spaces frightens me." (392), "Man is but a reed, the weakest thing in nature, but he is a thinking reed . . ."

6. *The Dignity of Man*—In the heart of this vast, oppressive universe, there is *man,* a being infinitely greater than the cosmos. . . . Why? "Because man resides in the mind of God, ceaselessly" the psalmist tells us. "What is man that you should keep him in mind, mortal man that you care for him?" For man, God has set aside a special favor which the celestial bodies have no need for: *Love . . .*

God Loves Man!

PSALM 15

יְהֹוָה מִי־יָגוּר בְּאׇהֳלֶךָ

LORD, WHO SHALL BE ADMITTED TO YOUR TENT?

1 Lord, who shall be admitted to your tent
and dwell on your holy mountain?

2 He who walks without fault;
he who acts with justice
and speaks the truth from his heart;
3 he who does not slander with his tongue;
he who does no wrong to his brother,
who casts no slur on his neighbour,
4 who holds the godless in disdain,
but honours those who fear the Lord;
he who keeps his pledge, come what may;
5 who takes no interest on a loan
and accepts no bribes against the innocent.
Such a man will stand firm for ever.

■

A MINI-DECALOGUE FOR THE GUEST OF THE LORD
or "The path that leads to God."

1. To live without fault . . .
2. To act with justice . . .
3. To speak the truth . . .
4. To be discreet . . .
5. To search for quality relationships . . .
6. To discern divine values . . .
7. To keep company with those who honor the Lord . . .

15

8. **To be faithful to the given word . . .**
9. **To resist the attraction of money . . .**
10. **To refuse bribes and corruption . . .**

Whoever Follows These Rules "Will Stand Firm Forever."

■

A FIRST READING: WITH ISRAEL

This is a "Psalm of Ascents." The Jews of Palestine would "go up" to Jerusalem once a year. These pilgrimages which punctuated the life of Jesus defined the most important time of the year, a time of renewal for all devout Jews. As soon as the pilgrims arrived in Jerusalem, their first visit was naturally to the temple.

Psalm 15 is part of the "catechesis at the door." Since pilgrims who came from far away may have been contaminated by pagan customs, the priests would give them religious instruction before allowing them into the holy place. The first verse of the psalm is the ritual question of a pilgrim: "Lord, who shall be admitted to your tent?" The rest of the psalm is the answer of the priests, in the form of a mini-decalogue. We are struck by the human character of these rules: In order to gain access to the Lord, we do not have to adhere to ritual precepts, or to liturgical or cultic rules. All we have to do is to follow a moral code of conduct, all we have to do is simply "be human." We must live blameless lives, be honest, just, truthful; we must stay away from the godless and keep the company of those who honor God. We must not be attached to material possessions and we must be willing to loan money without interest. We cannot let ourselves be corrupted by bribes.

In summary, all God expects from us is to maintain quality human relationships . . . a very modern concept indeed!

A SECOND READING: WITH JESUS

"Lord, who shall be admitted to your tent?" One day, a rich young man asked Jesus a similar question: ". . . What must I do to inherit eternal life?" And Jesus' response was to give him a moral code for life (Mk 10:17–19). We prepare ourselves to meet God by respecting our own human nature which was created by God.

In the concrete precepts of the gospel we find many parallels with this psalm: "Set your hearts on his kingdom first, and on God's saving justice . . ." (Mt 6:33)—"All you need say is 'Yes' if you mean yes, 'No' if you mean no." (Mt 5:37)—"No one can be the slave of two masters . . . you cannot be the slave both of God and of money" (Mt 6:24).

On an even deeper level, Jesus himself embodied the ideal given by this psalm: he *was* this "upright man" who dwells with God on his holy mountain.

A THIRD READING: WITH OUR TIME

1. *To Meet God. To Live With God. To Live Eternal Life*—Like the pilgrims in the temple, we are often tempted to think that it is in a temple that we will first meet God. But our Lord himself clearly reminded us of the importance of human relationships as being the first meeting place with him. Jesus told us emphatically: ". . . if you are bringing your offering to the altar and there remember that your brother has something against you, leave your offering there, before the altar, go and be reconciled with your brother first, and then come back and present your offering . . ." (Mt 5:23–24).

2. *A Simple Moral Code*—Nowadays, the idea of a moral code is very unpopular. Yet, what human society could possibly survive without a minimum set of rules, a basic consensus about good and evil? Let us for a moment imagine what a society without any moral code would be: a jungle in which injustice runs rampant, where people steal shamelessly, where people lie according to their opportunistic interests, where the strongest is always right, and where money is the supreme value.

When we pray this psalm we should simply pray that human beings conduct themselves as human beings should.

3. *Universal Salvation*—With the growing number of unbelievers and non-practicing Christians, we are faced with the question of eternal salvation: How does one gain access to the Life of God? How does one escape eternal damnation? Frightening is the formula of this psalm which asks us to "hold the godless in disdain." Our modern mindset rejects these abrupt classifications: How can *we* judge and decide that someone is evil, godless or reprobate? But the entire life of Jesus—the Son of God made flesh for all human beings and for their salvation —is living proof that God "wants every one to be saved" (1 Tm 2:4). It is not really God who "reprobates" man, it is man who

deliberately excludes himself from the salvific love of God. We can see from this psalm that all we as human beings need to do to enter the presence of God—whether believer or non-believer, whether atheist or pagan—is simply to live according to the universal rules of the human conscience.

Nevertheless, we Christians—more than anyone else—are called to this demanding life-style, according to the will of God, "since whoever does not love the brother whom he can see cannot love God whom he has not seen" (1 Jn 4:20). But simply leading a righteous life is not enough unless one also searches for the Lord in earnest.

There is no possible dichotomy between life and faith, and the ideal balance lies in the total unity between faith and daily life. Happy are those who believe, but they must also be just . . . Happy are the just, but they must also search for the truth!

4. *The Importance of "Tongue" and "Money"*—In this mini-decalogue, we are struck by the importance given to sins related to "tongue" and to money: If we are to truly love, we must learn how to control our tongues and be good stewards of our money.

PSALM 16

שָׁמְרֵנִי אֵל

LORD, MY PORTION

1 Preserve me, God, I take refuge in you.
2 I say to the Lord: "You are my God.
   My happiness lies in you alone."

3 All the idols of the land, these gods I have loved,
   continuously spread their destruction
   and people flock to them.*
4 Never will I offer their offerings of blood.
   Never will I take their name upon my lips.

5 O Lord, it is you who are my portion and my cup;
   it is you yourself who are my prize.
6 The lot marked out for me is my delight:
   welcome indeed the heritage that falls to me.

7 I will bless the Lord who gives me counsel,
   who even at night directs my heart.
8 I keep the Lord ever in my sight:
   since he is at my right hand, I shall stand firm.

9 And so my heart rejoices, my soul is glad;
   even my body shall rest in safety.
10 For you will not leave my soul among the dead,
   nor let your beloved know decay.

---

* For v. 3, the Grail version reads:
" He has put into my heart a marvellous love
   for the faithful ones who dwell in his land.
   Those who choose other gods increase their sorrows."

11 You will show me the path of life,
    the fullness of joy in your presence,
    at your right hand happiness for ever.

■

A PETITION: "PRESERVE ME!"
    —my God
    —my refuge
    —my happiness

A CHOICE, A RADICAL OPTION
    against false gods
    against paganism which spreads more and more
    an absolute rejection of any idol

INTIMACY WITH GOD BRINGS HAPPINESS
    I regret nothing
    I made a marvelous choice
    God is my counselor
    God is a constant presence watching over me
    God is my joy, my gladness
    God is my life, my resurrection
    God is the path and the meaning of my life
    God is my happiness forever

■

A FIRST READING: WITH ISRAEL

Here the psalmist lives in a materialistic world, in a society invaded by pagan cults: people worship idols and offer to them libations of blood, children are sacrificed to Moloch. The author denounces the extraordinary growth of paganism, its practices, and its ravages.

This man must have been tempted by those "other gods" but he converted to the true God. He resisted the temptation of *syncretism,* which is a combination of a little bit of faith with a lot of materialism, a little bit of true religion with a few idols, a little bit of God and a little bit of Mammon.

The psalmist, tempted and troubled by the world around him, comes to ask the Lord to throw light on the meaning of Israel's existence as "a separate people, a chosen people," yet he knows deep in his heart that he has the best lot in life. This demanding choice of a practicing believer is not a burden, a difficult duty, but rather an overflowing fountain of happiness that pagans cannot understand. The psalmist describes his life of communion with God, and the vocabulary of happiness bursts from his lips: my refuge, my inheritance, my cup, my prize, my delight, my joy, my happiness.

Verses 5 and 6 allude to the fact that when the Israelites divided the Promised Land, the Levites did not receive any territory. They were to serve God in his temple; Yahweh was their portion and their lot (Nb 18:20; Dt 10:9; Si 45:22). Thus the lives of the Levites, who lived in the temple, become a symbol of communion with God. The land of Canaan is the sacred domain of God, given to his people; the house of God is the sacred domain where he welcomes his guests. These are all prophetic signs of the messianic era when the Lord will dwell with his people and his people will dwell with him.

A SECOND READING: WITH JESUS

"You will not leave my soul among the dead, nor let your *beloved* (*hasid* in Hebrew) know decay." *Hasid* is one of these words which has no exact translation in English. The *hasid* is the person who is the object of the divine *hesed* or merciful love.

The person thus becomes one of the "faithful," one of the "friends" of God: he responds to love. *Jesus is the true "hasid."*

As a matter of fact, the only person who can now sing this psalm is the risen Christ who conquered death! Even in the darkness of the tomb, "my heart rejoices . . . my body shall rest in safety. . . ." You will not abandon me to death, you will not let "the one you love and who loves you know decay!" We do not know whether or not the psalmist was thinking about the doctrine of the resurrection, but he knew instinctively that one of the demands love puts upon us is not to accept being separated from the one we love: our belief in the resurrection is based upon this certitude—repeated a thousand times—that God loves us with merciful love (with *hesed.*)

"O Lord, it is you who are my portion and my cup." One day Jesus took a cup in his hands, and we in turn are also called to take it, following his command: "Take and drink." Yes, our destiny is wonderful, our lot is the best . . . and we continue to gather together to give thanks in the eucharist.

"The Lord is leading me . . . He is on my right. I find joy in his presence, happiness at his right hand." We can hear Jesus praying these heartfelt words. We sometimes wonder what Jesus was saying during the long nights *he* spent in prayer (Lk 6:12; Mt 5:1; Mk 3:13). Since he had been nourished by the psalms, he may have said this very psalm. So when we pray it, we pray the prayer of Jesus.

To express his communion with the Father, Jesus often used the image of the dwelling place, the house of God: "Remain in me, as I in you" (Jn 15:4); "Look, I am standing at the door, knocking. If one of you hears me calling and opens the door, I will come in to share a meal at that person's side" (Rv 3:20). It is not by chance that Jesus chose as a sign of his presence a meal to which he invites us!

A THIRD READING: WITH OUR TIME

1. *The Challenging Life of a True Believer*—Those who believe are men and women immersed in a world that lives according to different rules: "Here we are, fools for Christ's sake" (1 Co 4:10). Like the psalmist, we may feel very lonely at times. We are

surrounded by paganism and tempted by so many idols: money, possessions, sex, power, pleasure. If I take a close look at my personal life, I will discover my own private idol, the one meaningless thing which is so important to me. This psalm allows us to ask God that we may never "absolutize" anything. The only Absolute *is* God! Nobody and nothing else! If anything else becomes an absolute for me, it is an idol which will eventually crumble in my hands. Lord, deliver me from idols!

2. *The Certitude That God Is With Us—Emmanuel—*We can have ongoing communication with God, day and night, through meditation, conversation, and prayer. Others have chosen the idols of the world . . . Lord, give me the grace to choose *you,* and only you as my absolute love.

3. *The Theme of Happiness—*Let us listen to Paul Claudel's translation of this psalm: "Let me measure with awe this inheritance that came to me from heaven . . . You filled me to the brim with your presence . . . Listen to what I am telling you, in whispers so that only you can hear. O Master! I received so much without having to pay . . . O Wonder! The lot that befell me is truly amazing! The share I received is—without any doubt—marvelous! . . . You charmed my heart, you untied my tongue . . . Let *your face* fill me with delight, your face the vision of which is where all roads lead . . ."

With the help of this psalm, let us try to discover—with God—the language of the beloved, of the *hasidim.*

PSALM 17

שִׁמְעָה יְהוָה צֶדֶק

GUARD ME, O LORD!

1 Lord, hear a cause that is just,
   pay heed to my cry.
   Turn your ear to my prayer:
   no deceit is on my lips.

2 From you may my judgment come forth.
   Your eyes discern the truth.

3 You search my heart, you visit me by night.
   You test me and you find in me no wrong.
   My words are not sinful
4 As are men's words.

   I kept from violence because of your word,
5 I kept my feet firmly in your paths;
   there was no faltering in my steps.

6 I am here and I call, you will hear me, O God.
   Turn your ear to me; hear my words.
7 Display your great love, you whose right hand saves
   your friends from those who rebel against them.

8 Guard me as the apple of your eye.
   Hide me in the shadow of your wings
9 from the violent attack of the wicked.

   My foes encircle me with deadly intent.
10 Their hearts tight shut, their mouths speak proudly.
11 They advance against me, and now they surround me.

   Their eyes are watching to strike me to the ground
12 as though they were lions ready to claw

25

or like some young lion crouched in hiding.

13 Lord, arise, confront them, strike them down!
    Let your sword rescue my soul from the wicked;
14 let your hand, O Lord, rescue me from men,
    from men whose reward is in this present life.

    You give them their fill of your treasures;
    they rejoice in abundance of offspring
    and leave their wealth to their children.

15 As for me, in my justice I shall see your face
    and be filled, when I awake,
    with the sight of your glory.

■

LAMENT OF AN INNOCENT PERSON UNJUSTLY ACCUSED
Help me, O lord!
Render a just sentence!

YOU KNOW THAT I AM INNOCENT
I am here and I call . . .
Turn your ear to me . . .
Display your great love . . .
Save me . . .
Guard me . . .

SAVE ME FROM INJUSTICE

SAVE ME FROM MY FOES
They are wicked
**   arrogant**
**   murderous**

AND I SHALL LIVE IN COMMUNION WITH YOU . . .

■

A FIRST READING: WITH ISRAEL

We may at first feel uncomfortable with the protestations of innocence at the beginning of the psalm, and with the violent imprecations at the end. But let us try to understand the situation which gave rise to this psalm.

This man is innocent, his life is in danger; he has not committed any of the crimes he is accused of. . . . Have we become incapable of fighting for justice? Should Christian meekness—which is a duty—lead us to a kind of indifference to the evil that our brothers and sisters, and we ourselves, suffer?

Let us not forget that in addition to this individual oppressed by arrogant foes, we also have the collective situation of Israel (and of all humankind) in the clutches of the enemy, the ungodly, the accuser ("Satan" in Hebrew).

How beautiful is the reaction of this person, hunted down by his enemies, who comes to seek refuge in the temple. . . . Ancient societies possessed the admirable concept that places of worship were inviolate sanctuaries and that God was the defender and guarantor of justice.

Is it not normal for a person who is convinced of her innocence to call on the Lord's judgment? Deliver the sentence, O Lord! You alone know the truth.

A SECOND READING: WITH JESUS

There are some words in this psalm which only Jesus could possibly utter in truth. During his passion, *he* was truly the innocent man, unjustly accused. "You search my heart . . . you test me and you find in me no wrong . . . I kept my feet firmly in your paths; there was no faltering in my steps. Hide me . . . from the violent attack of the wicked . . . My foes encircle me with deadly intent . . . In your justice, I shall see your face and be filled, when I awake, with the sight of your glory."

Jesus did experience this awakening on Easter morning . . . and now he does see the face of God and can feast on the sight of his father's glory . . . forever!

However, instead of asking for the death of his enemies, Jesus prayed for them: "Father, forgive them; they do not know

what they are doing" (Lk 23:34). And when we read: "Hide me
in the shadows of your wings," we are irresistibly brought back
to one of Jesus' sayings: "How often have I longed to gather
your children together, as a hen gathers her chicks under her
wings . . ." (Mt 23:37).

A THIRD READING: WITH OUR TIME

1. *Justice And Injustice*—Even if these two words are ambigu-
ous and charged with ideological passion, we must recognize
that they refer to realities which men and women of today are
especially sensitive to. "Lord, hear a cause that is just," said the
psalmist. Let this be our prayer today!

2. *Revenge and Violence*—In today's world, there is a constant increase of violence: there seem to be more kidnappings,
more assaults, more hijackings and more gang warfare than ever
before. But if we take time to look at the history of humankind,
we will find that societies in ages past were not especially gentle
either . . . and the violent language of some psalms bears witness to far-away times when there was constant bloodshed. But
these verses which express hatred for enemies should remind us
who live in the twentieth century that many of our fellow human
beings are still being oppressed.

If the gospel asks us to be meek and peace-loving, it also
urges us to fight against evil and reminds us that "the kingdom of
Heaven has been subjected to violence and the violent are
taking it by storm" (Mt 11:12).

What the gospel challenges us to do—in imitation of Christ
—is to hate sins but love the sinner.

3. *Communion With God*—"Guard me as the apple of your
eye, hide me in the shadow of your wings. . . . I shall see your
face and be filled, when I awake, with the sight of your glory."
This is man's supreme reward. This is true and definitive justice.
In some extreme situations, living in profound communion with
God *is* the only efficacious attitude.

Let us remember those who are persecuted and tortured
and whose just cause may never be heard in this world.

4. *Awakening*—The last words of the psalm of "the perse-

cuted innocent" show us that this downtrodden person is filled with tranquil assurance: he is waiting for the Day of Judgment, and he knows that after the darkness of the night comes the awakening to a new life, a life in which justice will be restored.

Even if we don't feel any affinity with this psalm, let us pray for all who suffer injustice . . . and there are so many!

O Lord, hear the voice of justice! Turn your ear to those who suffer!

PSALM 19   הַשָּׁמַיִם מְסַפְּרִים כְּבוֹד־אֵל

THE HEAVENS PROCLAIM THE GLORY OF GOD

2   The heavens proclaim the glory of God
     and the firmament shows forth the work of his hands.
3   Day unto day takes up the story
     and night unto night makes known the message.

4   No speech, no word, no voice is heard
5   yet their span extends through all the earth,
     their words to the utmost bounds of the world.

     There he has placed a tent for the sun;
6   it comes forth like a bridegroom coming from his tent,
     rejoices like a champion to run its course.

7   And the end of the sky is the rising of the sun;
     to the furthest end of the sky is its course.
     There is nothing concealed from its burning heat.

*   *   *

8   The law of the Lord is perfect,
     it revives the soul.
     The rule of the Lord is to be trusted,
     it gives wisdom to the simple.

9   The precepts of the Lord are right,
     they gladden the heart.
     The command of the Lord is clear,
     it gives light to the eyes.

10   The fear of the Lord is holy,
     abiding for ever.

The decrees of the Lord are truth
and all of them are just.

11   They are more to be desired than gold,
than the purest gold
and sweeter are they than honey,
than honey from the comb.

12   So in them your servant finds instruction;
great reward is in their keeping.
13   But who can detect all his errors?
From hidden faults acquit me.

14   From presumption restrain your servant
and let it not rule me.
Then shall I be blameless,
clean from grave sin.

15   May the spoken words of my mouth,
the thoughts of my heart,
win favour in your sight, O Lord,
my rescuer, my rock!

■

A COSMIC HYMN
Praise be to the Creator!
the day sky: the light
the night sky: the stars

the heavens "speak"
yet their speech is silent,
understood by everybody,
beyond linguistic frontiers.

The Sun (the image of God)
—joyful
—active

—immense
—nothing is hidden from it

AN HISTORIC HYMN TO THE GOD OF THE COVENANT
The Law of the Lord is perfect
    —it is a source of life
        to be trusted
    —it gives wisdom
        it is upright
    —it rejoices the heart
        it is clear
    —it enlightens the eyes
        it is pure
    —it is a source of stability
        it is just
    —it is always valid
        it is to be desired—a sure value
        it is sweet

A PRAYER OF SUPPLICATION
Forgive my sins, O Lord
    —the deliberate ones
    —the ones I am not aware of
Let my life and my prayer be acceptable to you
O Lord, my rock and my redeemer. . . .

■

A FIRST READING: WITH ISRAEL

The two parts of the song are closely related: The God who created the physical laws of the universe is also the God who created the moral code of humankind. Thanks to this song, we enter into contact with the very soul of Israel, a people devoted to the Divine Law (the Torah) with a profound and sincere love. This admirable description of a cosmos which "speaks" to those who know how to admire it (the universe, the heavens, the stars and the sun) only serves as a preface to this incredible statement: God spoke to his people and revealed his thoughts to them. To a devout Jew, the Law, far from being a meddlesome hindrance or a legalistic, formalistic set of rules, is truly a gift from God. By revealing his laws to humankind, God made a covenant with us in order to help us in our daily lives. Just like the sun, which takes the earth as his bride in order to give her life, God gives the Law to his people in a joyful matrimonial celebration, a nuptial mystery. The qualities of the Law resemble the qualities lovers attribute to each other. Half of them are objective qualities which define the Law itself: perfect, trustworthy, upright, clear, pure, and just. The other half are subjective qualities which list the effects on men and women: the Law is a source of life, it gives wisdom, it gladdens the heart, and it enlightens the eyes.

A SECOND READING: WITH JESUS

Jesus must have prayed this psalm with special fervor . . . His parables, which almost always take their themes from nature, show us how much he admired creation, and how much the beauty of the universe must have spoken to him about his father!

As for Jesus' love of his father's will, the gospel is filled with it: "My food is to do my father's will." Modern men and women are astonished by this love for the Law, for we have come to dislike law, any law. Did we forget that there are "love laws? . . ." Did we forget that the only law is *love?* "I give you a new commandment: Love one another; you must love one another just as I have loved you" (Jn 13:34). Let us read again the praises of the Law which are at the heart of this psalm, while reflecting on this command of our Lord.

A THIRD READING: WITH OUR TIME

1. Contemporary philosophers have discovered the profound relationship that exists between man and nature. In one way, we are bound by the physical and chemical laws of the cosmos. We are, for instance, completely dependent upon the sun: if the sun ceased to warm the earth, all life would stop . . . Could there be a more beautiful metaphor for God than that of the sun? The psalmist who wrote this poem was surrounded by civilizations who worshipped the sun, and he may have borrowed the first part of the psalm from them. But he himself did not worship the sun, and his heart knew that the sun adores God and proclaims his glory.

We should meditate on this psalm in the countryside, on a beautiful spring day. Get up early to contemplate the rising sun, follow its dazzling circuit through the day, and witness the spectacular explosion of light at sunset . . . We should stay until night comes forth, spy the first stars kindling in the twilight and then, in the shades of night, let ourselves be overwhelmed by the star-studded firmament, the work of God's hands.

2. The author of this psalm could hear day and night communicating, back and forth, like two magnificent choirs echoing one another. Yes, the heavens do speak! What do they say? They proclaim the glory of God! How do they speak? In silence . . . "No speech, no word, no voice is heard." God speaks through silence: he speaks through creation, in a language which everybody can understand, for its message transcends the boundaries of languages. The fact that this great and marvelous God did not stop his creation with this magnificent symphony of the spheres, but that he also decided to make a covenant with us by giving us his Law, this should overwhelm us with love. . . . Clearly, *God is love*. To love is to follow the law of Christ—it is to be in harmony with the universe, united with God.

3. "Night unto night makes known the message." The light of the sun sings the glory of God, but with the psalmist, we must also discover the beauty of the night. The day is energy, action, life . . . The night is rest, peace, mystery . . . We should follow the Eastern example and learn how to empty ourselves, how to quiet the discordant voices within us, how to collect ourselves. This is the primary preparation for prayer. Of course, we can pray with your eyes open, but we should also experience prayer with our eyes closed, creating "night within our soul." According to St. John of the Cross, it is only "in the darkness of the night" that we can encounter God. Let us listen to a few stanzas from his "Song of the soul that is glad to know God by faith":

". . . This deathless spring is hidden. Even so
Full well I guess from whence its sources flow
Though it be night!

Its origin (since it has none) no one knows:
But that all origin from it arose
Although by night.

. . . The current that is nourished by this source
I know to be omnipotent in force
Although by night . . .

The eternal source hides in the Living Bread
That we with life eternal may be fed
Though it be night.*

4. *The Law of God*—We, men and women of today, must rediscover what a law is . . . It is clear that the psalmist finds great joy in the Law. He does not seem in the least constrained or coerced by it, as if it was imposed upon him from the outside . . . "The precepts of the Lord are right, they gladden the heart . . . they are more to be desired than gold, than the purest

---

* from *The Poems of St. John of the Cross,* Pantheon Books, Random House.

gold, and sweeter are they than honey." We know that no human group can function without laws. Without laws, we suffer war, injustice and anarchy. Without laws, there is no possibility for happiness; and no society can survive without a minimum of rules freely adopted and respected by all its members. The law of God is even more profound: it rules from within us, the good functioning of our being, to function well, for "the law of the Lord is perfect, it revives the soul. . . . Great reward is in its keeping."

PSALM 22   אֵלִי אֵלִי לָטָה עֲזַבְתָּנִי

MY GOD, WHY HAVE YOU FORSAKEN ME?

2 My God, my God, why have you forsaken me?
    You are far from my plea and the cry of my distress.

3 O my God, I call by day and you give no reply;
    I call by night and I find no peace.

4 Yet you, O God, are holy,
    enthroned on the praises of Israel.

5 In you our fathers put their trust;
    they trusted and you set them free.

6 When they cried to you, they escaped.
    In you they trusted and never in vain.

7 But I am a worm and no man,
    the butt of men, laughing-stock of the people.

8 All who see me deride me.
    They curl their lips, they toss their heads.

9 "He trusted in the Lord, let him save him;
    let him release him if this is his friend."

10 Yes, it was you who took me from the womb,
    entrusted me to my mother's breast.

11 To you I was committed from my birth,
    from my mother's womb you have been my God.

12 Do not leave me alone in my distress;
    come close, there is no one else to help.

13 Many bulls have surrounded me,
    fierce bulls of Bashan close me in.

14 Against me they open wide their jaws,
    like lions, rending and roaring.

15   Like water I am poured out,
       disjointed are all my bones.
       My heart has become like wax,
       it is melted within my breast.

16   Parched as burnt clay is my throat,
       my tongue cleaves to my jaws.
17   Many dogs have surrounded me,
       a band of the wicked beset me.
       They tear holes in my hands and feet
       and lay me in the dust of death.

18   I can count every one of my bones.
       These people stare at me and gloat;
19   they divide my clothing among them.
       They cast lots for my robe.

20   O Lord, do not leave me alone,
       my strength, make haste to help me!
21   Rescue my soul from the sword,
       my life from the grip of these dogs.
22   Save my life from the jaws of these lions,
       my poor soul from the horns of these oxen.

       You have answered my plea, O Lord!*
23   I will tell of your name to my brethren
       and praise you where they are assembled.
24   "You who fear the Lord give him praise;
       all sons of Jacob, give him glory.
       Revere him, Israel's sons.

25   For he has never despised
       nor scorned the poverty of the poor.
       From him he has not hidden his face,
       but he heard the poor man when he cried.
26   You are my praise in the great assembly.

---

* This verse is not in the Grail version.

My vows I will pay before those who fear him.
27 The poor shall eat and shall have their fill.
They shall praise the Lord, those who seek him.
May their hearts live for ever and ever!

28 All the earth shall remember and return to the Lord,
all families of the nations worship before him
29 for the kingdom is the Lord's; he is ruler of the nations.
30 They shall worship him, all the mighty of the earth;
before him shall bow all who go down to the dust.

31 And my soul shall live for him, my children serve him.
They shall tell of the Lord to generations yet to come,
32 declare his faithfulness to peoples yet unborn:
"These things the Lord has done."

■

**All Christians know—or should know—the four Hebrew
words: "Eli, eli lama tsabachtani . . ." These are the very words
Christ shouted just before his death. . . . Our dying Lord prayed
this psalm which expresses both facets of the great mystery of
love: the most dismal dereliction of Good Friday as well as the
most triumphant prayer of thanksgiving of Easter Sunday.**

LAMENTATION:

> **SPIRITUAL SUFFERING**
> **God is silent . . . "You are far away . . ."**
> **Yet, there is comfort in the midst of affliction**
> **Men scorn me . . .**
> **Yet, there is absolute trust**

PRAYER:

> **Do not leave me alone . . .**
> **Wild beasts symbolizing evil . . .**

PHYSICAL SUFFERING
—dislocated limbs
—anguish, prostration
—parching thirst
—bleeding hands and feet
—bones protruding
   under the distended flesh
—clothing drawn by lot
—coup de grâce of the sword

THANKSGIVING: "You have answered my plea!"
   With Israel: praise
               the meal of the poor
   With all of humankind: the kingdom of God
               eternal life

■

A FIRST READING: WITH ISRAEL

As paradoxical as it may seem, this is a psalm of thanksgiving, and its essential meaning is given in the last words. The psalmist sings the song of thanksgiving of Israel, "resurrected" after her return from exile. How moving it is to realize that the poet uses the image of somebody "crucified and brought back to life" to describe the liberation of his people!

A SECOND READING: WITH JESUS

Jesus did experience all the sufferings described by the psalmist: the anguish, the torture, the thirst caused by dehydration, the disjointed limbs, the blood pouring out of his hands and feet, the coup de grâce of the lance, the clothing divided among the executioners, the insults of his accusers.

The first part is a lamentation and it expresses such agonizing and realistic suffering that it is almost unbearable. We can admire the beauty of this "man of sorrows," but unlike Jeremiah in his Laments, Jesus did not show any anger or utter any curses against his tormentors. He did moan in pain, but he did so with a kind of profound peace in which some rays of hope are already mingled: "Yet you, O God, are holy . . . in you our fathers put their trust . . . it was you who took me from the womb, entrusted me to my mother's breast . . . from my mother's womb you have been my God." Jesus did not question the philosophical significance of evil: he suffered, that is all, and because of his agony, he just prayed with even more intensity.

If we follow the rhythm of the psalm, we can penetrate into the depths of Jesus' soul: "You are far . . . Do not leave me alone in my distress . . . You have answered my plea." Resurrection, glory and praise were in Jesus' heart, even as he was nailed to the cross.

Let us—slowly—read again the third section of the psalm, putting it on the lips of the crucified Lord. It is truly an outburst of thanksgiving (*eucharistia* in Greek). Let us not forget that the day before he died, Jesus had "rehearsed" his death and given thanks with the paschal meal. He did know the extraordinary fecundity of his sacrifice, and he was inviting his brothers and sisters to a meal where "the poor shall eat and shall have their fill," so that they could sing the praises of the Father with him. "These things the Lord has done." And we reenact this meal in each one of our eucharistic celebrations.

A THIRD READING: WITH OUR TIME

"Why have you forsaken me? . . ." This is a prayer that we all can say . . . But, let us say it to the end and add: "They shall praise the Lord, those who seek him. May their hearts live for ever and ever. . . . And my soul shall live for him . . . These things the Lord has done!"

PSALM 24 לַיהוָה הָאָרֶץ וּמְלוֹאָהּ

HE IS THE KING OF GLORY!

1 The Lord's is the earth and its fullness,
 the world and all its peoples.
2 It is he who set it on the seas;
 on the waters he made it firm.

3 Who shall climb the mountain of the Lord?
 Who shall stand in his holy place?
4 The man with clean hands and pure heart,
 who does not sell his soul to idols*
 (who has not sworn so as to deceive his neighbour.)

5 He shall receive blessings from the Lord
 and reward from the God who saves him.
6 Such are the men who seek him,
 seek the face of the God of Jacob.

* * *

7 O gates, lift high your heads;
 grow higher, ancient doors.
 Let him enter, the king of glory!

8 Who is the king of glory?
 The Lord, the mighty, the valiant,
 the Lord, the valiant in war.

9 O gates, lift high your heads;
 grow higher, ancient doors.
 Let him enter, the king of glory!

---

* For v. 4, the Grail version reads:
 ". . . who desires not worthless things."

10   Who is he, the king of glory?
     He, the Lord of armies,
     he is the king of glory.

■

A PROCESSIONAL HYMN
in honor of the Creator of the universe

A QUESTION IN FRONT OF THE TEMPLE GATES: WHO SHALL ENTER?
—**pure heart**
—**innocent hands**
—**loyalty . . . justice**
—**seeking the face of God**
—**freedom from idols**

A TRIUMPHANT ENTRY INTO THE HOLY PLACE
The pilgrims, with lyrical enthusiasm,
invite the gates to "grow higher"

God is coming: the King of Glory!
                the Lord of armies!

■

A FIRST READING: WITH ISRAEL

This "Psalm of Kingship" describes a procession entering the temple. It is Yahweh, the creator of the universe, it is Yahweh, our king, who comes to take possession of his city and of his palace. How does God reign? At the temple door the "catechists" would answer that the King of Glory comes through the moral conduct of the lives of men and women who have pure hearts and keep their hands clean from dishonest dealings, who do not "sell their souls to idols," who are detached from anything that is not God, true to their word, hungry for justice and thirsty for the knowledge of God. When the procession arrives at the front court of the temple, we have a dialogue between the faithful who want to gain admission and the guardians of the temple whose duty it is to preserve the sacred character of this holy place. Then the crowd addresses the gates directly, personifying them, and shouts: "Open up, gates!" It is amazing that the worshippers command the gateposts not only to spread apart (as would be normal) but also to raise themselves: "Grow higher, ancient doors!" The gates are asked to perform this symbolical gesture of homage, in order to underline the majesty of the king who is going to enter through them.

A SECOND READING: WITH JESUS

One day, just before his passion, Jesus willingly played the identical role of the king as described in this psalm. After leaving Bethany, a few miles from Jerusalem, with the acclamations of the crowds, he arrived in the city and went all the way to the Royal Portico, for this was a royal entry, the messianic entrance of the son of David, the "King of Israel" (Jn 12:13). John, who witnessed this short-lived triumph, emphasized this theme of the kingship of Jesus. In front of Pilate Jesus claimed his royal title: "Mine is not a kingdom of this world . . . I came into this world for this, to bear witness to the truth . . ." (Jn 18:36–37). And "Pilate wrote out a notice and had it fixed to the cross; it ran: "Jesus the Nazarene, King of the Jews" (Jn 19:19). The inscription lays emphasis on the fact that the cross is his real throne, the true majesty of the King of Glory; and the cross represents his infinite love, his sacrificial love.

Once more, we can truly say this psalm "with Jesus," for nobody more than Jesus could have lived it with more truth. It is as if this page from the Old Testament had been written just for him. "Who shall climb the mountain of the Lord?" Jesus shall indeed! Jesus, the man with the pure heart and innocent hands; Jesus, who never sold his soul to the idols of this world; Jesus who said "yes" when he meant "yes" and "no" when he meant "no" (Mt 5:37); Jesus who never swore "so as to deceive his neighbor"; Jesus who was a "blessing from the Lord and a reward from God"; Jesus who did "seek the face of the God of Jacob," the face of his Father, during his prayer-filled nights. As Paul said: "Jesus *is* the King of Glory" (1 Co 2:8).

And these doors which grow higher—against all the laws of nature—suggest the mysterious and sacred character of his resurrection and triumphant entry—no longer temporary but definitive this time—his entry into eternal glory. Yes, *he* is "The Lord, the mighty, the valiant in war," for "he is to be king until he has made his enemies his footstool, and the last of the enemies to be done away with is death . . ." (1 Co 15:25).

A THIRD READING: WITH OUR TIME

1. *The Freedom of the Christian Confronted with Earthly Realities*—Paul explicitly applied this psalm to a controversial issue of his time: Is it permissible to eat food sacrificed to idols? Paul answered: "Eat anything that is sold in butchers' shops: there is no need to ask questions for conscience's sake, since *to the Lord belong the earth and all it contains*" (1 Co 10:25–26; Ps 24:1).

This idea that faith in God brings freedom corresponds to one of the concerns of our contemporary society. Only God is God, only God deserves submission. We have a tendency to abusively "sacralize" earthly realities, traditional customs, or ancestral taboos. But today the greatest danger resides in the sacralization of our political and philosophical ideas, for we inject into them an absolute which only God possesses, for *he* is the only king.

2. *Faith and Ethics*—These two realities have been opposed in recent times. Psalm 24 reminds us of an essential truth which Jesus so often repeated: God demands more than ritual

acclamations or cultic gestures from us—he demands a right-eous life. Moral conscience comes first, and it is on love that we will be judged (Mt 25:31–46). "Who shall climb the mountain of the Lord?" It is not anyone who says . . . "Lord, Lord" (Mt 7:21), but those who will have kept their hearts pure and their hands clean by fulfilling the duties demanded by the dignity of the human condition. Who shall come near God? Whoever has purified himself of any conscious or unconscious fault, whoever has decided to fight against egotism, and against any form of idolatry. God is thus the guarantor of human dignity and con-science. When we proclaim: "Thy Kingdom come!" we commit ourselves to making it happen by living according to certain demanding rules.

3. *All Saints*—This psalm is sung on All Saints Day . . . Who can enter the heavens, the holy place of God? All the men and women who have fashioned their lives according to moral con-science and true love. You are *Love*, O Lord! Make us worthy to take part in your holiness.

PSALM 25

אֵלֶיךָ יְהוָה נַפְשִׁי

IN YOUR LOVE REMEMBER ME

1 To you, O Lord, I lift up my soul.
2 I trust you, let me not be disappointed;
    do not let my enemies triumph.
3 Those who hope in you shall not be disappointed,
    but only those who wantonly break faith.

4 Lord, make me know your ways.
    Lord, teach me your paths.
5 Make me walk in your truth, and teach me;
    for you are my God my saviour.

    In you I hope all day long
7c because of your goodness, O Lord.
6 Remember your mercy, Lord,
    and the love you have shown from of old.
7 Do not remember the sins of my youth.
    In your love remember me.

8 The Lord is good and upright.
    He shows the path to those who stray,
9 He guides the humble in the right path;
    He teaches his way to the poor.

10 His ways are faithfulness and love
    for those who keep his covenant and will.
11 Lord, for the sake of your name
    forgive my guilt; for it is great.

12 If anyone fears the Lord
    he will show him the path he should choose.
13 His soul shall live in happiness
    and his children shall possess the land.

14 The Lord's friendship is for those who revere him;
    to them he reveals his covenant.

15 My eyes are always on the Lord;
    for he rescues my feet from the snare.
16 Turn to me and have mercy
    for I am lonely and poor.

17 Relieve the anguish of my heart
    and set me free from my distress.
18 See my affliction and my toil
    and take all my sins away.

19 See how many are my foes;
    how violent their hatred for me.
20 Preserve my life and rescue me.
    Do not disappoint me, you are my refuge.
21 May innocence and uprightness protect me;
    for my hope is in you, O Lord.

22 Redeem Israel, O God, from all its distress.

■

Twenty pressing demands . . . asking God for:

THE GIFT OF FAITHFULNESS TO THE COVENANT
  Reasons for hope "coming from God":
      —your goodness . . .
      —your mercy . . .

THE FORGIVENESS OF UNFAITHFULNESS TO THE COVENANT
  Your love . . .
  Your holy name . . .
  Reasons for hope "coming from Man":
      I am lonely . . .

I am poor . . .
I am unhappy . . .
my affliction . . .
my toil . . .
my distress . . .
my sins . . .
my enemies . . .

Yes, Lord, I Hope in You, I Await Your Coming.

Save Us From Our Distress!

■

A FIRST READING: WITH ISRAEL

Like eight other psalms, psalm 25 is an alphabetical psalm: each verse starts with one of the letters of the Hebrew alphabet. This is not only a mnemonic and didactic device, but also a symbolical device used to express the "plenitude of the Law." Yes, the law of God is the perfection of the word from beginning to end. The acrostic form does, however, give a somewhat artificial style to the logical development of the hymn, and the poet's thoughts do not seem to follow a rigorous plan. But what a power of incantation there is in these twenty supplications expressed in twenty-two verses!

1. "Let me not be disappointed . . ."
2. "Do not let my enemies triumph . . ."
3. "Make me know your ways . . ."
4. "Teach me your paths . . ."
5. "Make me walk in your truth . . ."
6. "Teach me: for you are my God . . ."
7. "Remember your mercy . . . and your love . . ."
8. "Do not remember the sins of my youth . . ."
9. "In your love remember me . . ."
10. "Forgive my guilt; for it is great . . ."
11. "Turn to me . . ."
12. "Have mercy . . ."
13. "Relieve the anguish of my heart . . ."
14. "See my affliction and my toil . . ."
15. "Take all my sins away . . ."
16. "See how many are my foes . . ."
17. "Preserve my life . . ."
18. "Rescue me . . ."
19. "Do not disappoint me . . ."
20. "Redeem Israel . . ."

Twenty requests . . . twenty imperative demands addressed to God . . . twenty audacious petitions . . . twenty signs of confidence . . .

A SECOND READING: WITH JESUS

Jesus is the *One* who saves . . . He is the *One* who forgives our sins, and he presents himself as "the Way" to his Father. In this psalm, the words "paths of God" are used four times, the word *way* is used twice, and twice the poet asks the Lord to *guide us.* Yes, Lord Jesus, guide us, show us your way, *Be* our way . . . This psalm is the prayer of the *humble,* the *anawim,* and we know the place they held in Jesus' thoughts.

A THIRD READING: WITH OUR TIME

The two themes interwoven in this psalm are still very much up-to-date for any true Christian: (1) Grant us, O Lord, the *grace* to be *faithful* to your Covenant, and (2) grant us *forgiveness* for being *unfaithful* to your Covenant.

1. *Faithfulness to God—Faith*—is a type of superior wisdom, a way of life, the path to happiness. Let us meditate on this beautiful image of the path: we must go on, we must continue our journey "on the path of God."

2. *Hope in God*—The promised salvation is God himself! "Those who hope in *you* shall not be disappointed . . . In *you* I hope all day long . . . For my hope is in *you,* O Lord!" We can see why the church uses this psalm on the first Sunday of Advent. It is the Advent of the world which hopes that the promises of God will be fulfilled! It is the expectation and the longing for Christmas. Millions of poor have said this prayer in Old Testament times: "My hope is in *you.*" They did not know then how completely God was going to answer their prayers, by coming to earth himself, through the power of the Incarnation.

3. *Our Affliction*—We do not have to forget our sufferings in order to pray. On the contrary, the Bible teaches us to use them in order to "implore" like a beggar who is showing his wounds, telling the Lord: "See my misery and my pain . . . Look at my sins . . . Have mercy on me!" What was the exact nature of the affliction the psalmist endured? We do not know, but we understand that he was surrounded by wicked foes, and the striking metaphor of the snare in which he is caught reminds us of the hopeless situations in which we are sometimes ensnared.

The psalmist dared say: "Lord, rescue my feet from the snare!" We too can say this prayer with him.

4. *God Is Our Ally*—It is startling to see how in this psalm God does not behave like a judge confronting the sinner. Rather he is his advocate, his ally.

"I trust you . . . Do not let my enemies triumph . . . Do not remember the sins of my youth . . . He rescues my feet from the snare . . ." This concept of God is very modern, and we no longer accept the idea of a God of revenge as our ancestors did. The entire Old Testament speaks to us of a God who makes a covenant with Man, and who remains faithful even when Man rejects him. God suffers with us when we suffer because of our sin, and he commits himself—with all his might—to help us get through it. In the psalms, every time we see the word "enemy," we also see that God enlists himself on the side of his faithful in order to fight with them.

5. *Forgiveness*—There are three requests for forgiveness in this psalm: "Do not remember the sins of my youth . . . Forgive my guilt; for it is great . . . take all my sins away." What a positive attitude! This psalm reminds us that God is aware of how hard it is for us to do good and that he knows that we often sin out of weakness. But the very notion of sin is that it is "that which God forgives . . ." God likes to forgive us! God always forgives us as soon as we take the slightest step towards him. Is it surprising then that he expects that same attitude from us, so that we may be like him?

"Forgive us our trespasses as we forgive those who trespass against us."

PSALM 27

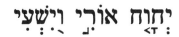

MY LIGHT AND MY HELP

1 The Lord is my light and my help;
   whom shall I fear?
   The Lord is the stronghold of my life;
   before whom shall I shrink?

2 When evil-doers draw near
   to devour my flesh.
   it is they, my enemies and foes,
   who stumble and fall.

3 Though an army encamp against me
   my heart would not fear.
   Though war break out against me
   even then would I trust.

4 There is one thing I ask of the Lord,
   for this I long,
   to live in the house of the Lord,
   all the days of my life,
   to savour the sweetness of the Lord,
   to behold his temple.

5 For there he keeps me safe in his tent
   in the day of evil.
   He hides me in the shelter of his tent,
   on a rock he sets me safe.

6 And now my head shall be raised
   above my foes who surround me
   and I shall offer within his tent
   a sacrifice of joy.
   I will sing and make music for the Lord.

7 O Lord, hear my voice when I call;
    have mercy and answer.
8 Of you my heart has spoken:
    "Seek his face."

    It is your face, O Lord, that I seek;
9 hide not your face.
    Dismiss not your servant in anger;
    you have been my help.

    Do not abandon or forsake me,
    O God my help!
10 Though father and mother forsake me,
    The Lord will receive me.

11 Instruct me, O Lord, in your way;
    on an even path lead me.
12 When they lie in ambush protect me
    from my enemy's greed.
    False witnesses rise against me,
    breathing out fury.

13 I am sure I shall see the Lord's goodness
    in the land of the living.
14 Hope in him, hold firm and take heart.
    Hope in the Lord!

■

TRIUMPHANT TRUST
    God my light
    God my salvation
    God my stronghold

VALIANT TRUST
    This is not complacent, naive optimism:
    The psalmist is in the thick of battle . . .
    but he confronts his enemy,

by relying not on his own strength,
but on the Lord's . . .

ONLY ONE DESIRE: COMMUNION WITH GOD

To be the guest of the Lord,
to dwell in his house,
where battles subside
where the Lord, my trust, resides.

sheltered by God . . .
hidden in God . . .
set safe on a rock . . .

I shall celebrate the eucharist, a festive sacrifice . . .
I shall sing . . .

IMPLORING TRUST

But alas, the peaceful interlude is short-lived.
Life goes on, and so does the warfare.
And once more the prayer becomes a breathless plea.

—listen to me . . .
—answer me . . .
—do not hide your face from me . . .
—do not dismiss me . . .
—do not forsake me . . .
—do not abandon me . . .
—lead me to safety . . .
—show me your path . . .
—protect me from the powers of evil . . .

SERENE CONCLUSION

Eschatological hope:
One day I shall see *you!*
Hope, O my soul!
Take heart!

■

A FIRST READING: WITH ISRAEL

This is a "psalm of trust" which may have been written for two different occasions. But we can nevertheless take note of the admirable movement of the psalmist's feelings (as outlined in the summary): (1) an affirmation of faith: God is salvation; (2) a nuance: this salvation implies our participation, and our courageous fight; (3) this courage finds its strength in one source: prayer; (4) life is still there, pressing, full of conflicts; but (5) the end of the prayer is filled anew with an unshakable trust in God.

Let us take note of the striking change of personal pronouns in verse 7: until then the psalmist had been talking *about* God in the third person. All of a sudden, he starts talking *to* God in the second person: "O Lord, hear my voice when I call . . ."

A SECOND READING: WITH JESUS

Once more, we discover that Jesus prayed this psalm. Here are a few moving allusions:

—"Evil-doers draw near to devour my flesh . . ."—the scourging and the passion.

—"False witnesses rise against me . . ."—(Mt 26:59).

—"To live in the house of the Lord" reminds us of Jesus' longing to remain in the temple on his first pilgrimage to Jerusalem: "Did you not know that I must be in my Father's house?" (Lk 2:49). The child Jesus had been molded by the longing expressed by the psalmist to "live in the house of the Lord," and he fulfilled his longing at the first opportunity.

—"There is one thing I ask of the Lord . . ."—"Set your heart on his kingdom first . . ." (Mt 6:33).

—"Before whom shall I shrink? . . ."—"There is no need to be afraid, little flock, for it has pleased your Father to give you the kingdom" (Lk 12:32).

—"Though war break out against me, even then would I trust . . ."—"The gates of the underworld can never over-power (my community)" (Mt 16:18).

—"Though father and mother forsake me, the Lord will receive me." When Jesus is left without any human support, he says: "The time will come . . . when you are going to be . . .

leaving me alone. And yet I am not alone, because the Father is with me" (Jn 16:32).—". . . because I am not alone: the one who sent me is with me" (Jn 8:16).—"He who sent me is with me, and has not left me to myself" (Jn 8:29).

—"The Lord is my light . . ."—". . . the light has come into the world" (Jn 3:19).—"I am the light of the world" (Jn 8:12, 12:46).

—"I shall see the Lord's goodness in the land of the living."—This is the antiphon of the mass for the dead, which expresses the certitude of the resurrection. "I am going to the Father" (Jn 14:28).

A THIRD READING: WITH OUR TIME

1. *The Theme of Hope*—Hope is one of the spiritual attitudes most needed in our modern world. But hope is not an easy or soothing virtue. It is, rather, an attitude that requires courage and strength. It is not only a human virtue, but also a theological virtue which takes root in prayer and in the desire for communion with God.

2. *The Theme of Crisis*—Our world is in crisis; our church is in crisis. The hope expressed by the psalmist is a "breathless" hope: fear is at the door, the war has erupted.

3. *The Eschatological Theme*—God will triumph in the end, and Paul reminds us that we shall indeed "see the Lord's goodness," that we shall see his face (1 Co 13:12). But this "light" and this "salvation" we are headed for are already in progress, and it is our duty as human beings to participate in it. "Hope in him, hold firm and take heart." This means: We can count on God, but we must also take action . . . Grace and freedom . . .

4. *The Theme of Prayer*—This psalm can provide us with the opportunity to experience once more—and on a deeper level—communion with God. The psalmist envisioned himself as the guest of God: "There is one thing I ask of the Lord, for this I long, to live in the house of the Lord, all the days of my life . . . he hides me in the shelter of his tent . . . It is your face, O Lord, that I seek . . ." Why don't we also try to experience the sweet presence of God? Did not Jesus (in line with this psalm) invite us to this intimate form of prayer: "When you pray, go to your

private room, shut yourself in, and so pray to your Father who is in that secret place . . ." (Mt 6:6). This is exactly what the psalmist said: "He hides me in the shelter of his tent." O, to hide in God, to bury oneself in God . . . Tenderly.

5. *The Theme of the "Face of God"*—Our contemporary western world is truly traumatized by the apparent absence of God, by the "silence" of God, which has led so many people to the conclusion that God does not exist, that "God is dead." "It is your face, O Lord, that I seek." Like us, the poet of long ago must have experienced the difficulty of meeting God, but his inner song ends in a cry of faith: "I am sure I shall see the Lord's goodness."

6. *The Theme of Daily Fight*—We should not be fooled by the intimate tone of this psalm of trust. Praying, dwelling in the house of the Lord, and seeking his face absolutely do not justify an egotistic flight from reality! The entire psalm is permeated with an atmosphere of warfare and tells us that seeking the face of God also implies fighting against evil.

PSALM 29

הָבוּ לַיהוָה כָּבוֹד

THE LORD'S VOICE

1 O give the Lord you sons of God,
   give the Lord glory and power;
2 give the Lord the glory of his name.
   Adore the Lord in his holy court.

3 The Lord's voice resounding on water,
   the Lord on the immensity of waters;
4 the voice of the Lord, full of power,
   the voice of the Lord, full of splendour.

5 The Lord's voice shattering the cedars,
   the Lord shatters the cedars of Lebanon;
6 he makes Lebanon leap like a calf
   and Sirion like a young wild-ox.

7 (The Lord's voice flashes flames of fire.)

8 The Lord's voice shaking the wilderness,
   the Lord shakes the wilderness of Kadesh;
9 The Lord's voice makes the hind to calve
   and strips the forest bare.*

3b The God of glory thunders.
10 In his temple they all cry: "Glory!"
    The Lord sat enthroned over the flood;
    the Lord sits as king for ever.

---

* For v 9, the Grail version reads:
  "The Lord's voice rending the oak tree
  and stripping the forest bare."

11   The Lord will give strength to his people,
     the Lord will bless his people with peace.

■

A Theophany of Yahweh:
   The Storm . . . *glory*
                 power
                 amazement

A STORM IN THE WEST, over the Mediterranean Sea
   the waters are "overpowered"

A STORM IN THE NORTH, over Lebanon
   the mountains are "shaken"

A STORM IN THE SOUTH, over the Negeb desert
   the animals are "panic-stricken"

But there is no fear in Israel . . .

In the temple, they all cry: "Glory! Yahweh is King!"

■

A FIRST READING: WITH ISRAEL

We have here an admirable piece of poetry: the description of a storm which starts over the sea in the west, moves to the north (the Lebanon and Sirion mountains), and finally reaches the desert of Kadesh in the south, surrounding all of Palestine. This description is very concrete: in the awesome flashes of lightning, the poet, led by his exalted imagination, sees the mountains leaping like furious bulls. The forests are struck down by thunderbolts and the towering trees are uprooted and crushed to the ground. The frightened animals come to be in labor before their time. These spectacular events are described with extremely simple literary devices: the same words are repeated following a gradual rhythm, like the rumbling of a prolonged echo; short, jerky sentences are used, and the entire poem is punctuated by *seven* claps of thunder: *the voice of the Lord* (In Hebrew *Qol Yahweh*).

In the Jewish liturgy, this psalm is sung on the feast of Pentecost which commemorates the *revelation on Mount Sinai.* The people of Israel remember this awesome theophany that they experienced during their forty years in the desert of Kadesh. To them the "voice of the Lord" which revealed the Law to his people did sound like thunder. It is not by chance that the voice of the Lord is heard *seven* times. Seven is a symbolic number, which represents perfection. The voice of the Lord *is* perfect!

This is one of the "Psalms of Kingship." The Lord sits as king for ever. The word *glory* (*Kabod* in Hebrew) is repeated four times . . . The word *Yahweh* (which we translate by *Lord*) is the "proper name" of God which, out of respect, the Jews never utter and which they replace by *Adonai.* The name Yahweh recurs eighteen times in this psalm, in almost every verse! God literally "fills" this psalm!

This divine storm is symbolical: Yahweh is the *victor over the forces of evil which threaten Israel.* All the pagan nations around are ravaged and devastated by the divine hurricane, leaving the people of Israel in peace so that they can proclaim the glory of God in his temple. These forces of evil are the demonic forces that threaten the people of God unceasingly.

They are the gods who have usurped the glory of the true God, but will be forced to return it to him.

A SECOND READING: WITH JESUS

The church suggests that we use this psalm on the Sunday of the Baptism of the Lord, when "the heavens opened . . . and suddenly there was a *voice* from heaven. This is my son . . ." (Jn 3:16–17). The gospel naturally used the cultural background of the people among whom it was first announced, and for a Jew of that time the thunder *was* the "voice of God." Saint John does not hesitate to tell us: "*A voice came from heaven*, 'I have glorified it, and I will again glorify it.' The crowd standing by, who heard this, said it was a clap of thunder; others said, It was an angel speaking to him" (Jn 12:28–29). In Revelation, the same John again heard "seven claps of thunder" (Rv 10:4), just like in this psalm. Let us ask ourselves why, on Pentecost Day, the coming of God was experienced as a storm which shook the house where the apostles were gathered (Ac 2:1–2) and why Saul was knocked down by a flash of lightning on his way to Damascus (Ac 9:3–4).

A THIRD READING: WITH OUR TIME

1. *Communion with the Great Forces of Nature Which Lie Beyond Our Comprehension*—We now know that storms follow some well-defined rules and that lightning is nothing more than electricity. Is it not healthy for us—in spite of this knowledge—to rediscover our insignificance in the face of the unleashing of the cosmic powers? Why could a storm not speak to us about God? Is speaking about the "voice" of God only a metaphor? Whoever has experienced a storm in the mountains is not likely to ever forget its solemn beauty! And the encounter with God can be experienced as a striking, dazzling thunderstorm (Paul's experience on the road to Damascus). Some recent converts have used the same language to relate their encounter with God.

2. *We Must Remain Men and Women of Peace in the Midst of Human Terrors and Trepidations*—At the very moment when

everything is "shaking" all around Israel, the faithful are peace-fully singing the glory of God in his temple, under the protection of the Lord who gives strength and blessings to his people. All we have to do is open our eyes and our ears to realize that although we have freed ourselves of some of the fears which haunted our ancestors, we have replaced them with new fears: the fear of atomic war, the fear of the future, the fear of the deterioration of nature, and the social fears of all kinds (injustice, unemployment, etc.).

Perhaps, praying this psalm *today* means that we have to draw ourselves up with courage; believing that people of *faith* should not be afraid of anything . . . for everything is in the hand of God! Let us not forget that Jesus gave John the nickname *Boarneges* or *Son of Thunder* (Mk 3:17). Tortured and exiled to the island of Patmos, John continued to sing the glory of God. He was definitely not a weakling! Such are men and women of faith. . . .

3. *Certitude of God's Final Victory*—The metaphor of the storm which "shatters the cedars" and "shakes the wilderness" reminds us that God will have the last word against all hostile forces. Jesus Christ is the *King of Glory* exalted by the psalmist. He is truly the *Lord's Voice,* his triumphant word. He is the Lord who—like a fire—"will destroy (sin) with the breath of his mouth" (1 Th 2:8). Let us rejoice!

May All Our Liturgies Be An Uninterrupted Cry: Glory!

PSALM 30

אֲרוֹמִמְךָ יְהוָה

YOU HAVE HEALED ME

2   I will praise you, Lord, you have rescued me
and have not let my enemies rejoice over me.

*   *   *

3   O Lord, I cried to you for help
and you, my God, have healed me.
4   O Lord, you have raised my soul from the dead,
restored me to life from those who sink into the grave.

5   Sing psalms to the Lord, you who love him,
give thanks to his holy name.
6   His anger lasts a moment; his favour all through life.
At night there are tears, but joy comes with dawn.

7   I said to myself in my good fortune:
"Nothing will ever disturb me."
8   Your favour had set me on a mountain fastness,
then you hid your face and I was put to confusion.

9   To you, Lord, I cried,
to my God I made appeal:
10 "What profit would my death be, my going to the grave?
Can dust give you praise or proclaim your truth?"

11 The Lord listened and had pity.
The Lord came to my help.
12 For me you have changed my mourning into dancing,
you removed my sackcloth and girded me with joy.
13 So my soul sings psalms to you unceasingly.
O Lord my God, I will thank you for ever.

■

A PRAYER OF THANKSGIVING

I WAS IN MORTAL DANGER . . .
   —too self-confident,
   —I experienced my weakness

I CRIED TO YOU, I IMPLORED YOU . . .

NOW, I GIVE THANKS TO YOU

■

A FIRST READING: WITH ISRAEL

This is a psalm of *todah,* of joyous thanksgiving, of eucharist. The words "give thanks" are used three times, and they are the final words of the psalm. There is a wealth of expressions of joy: "sing psalms" (twice), "joy," "good fortune," "dancing," "girded with joy."

Here is the concrete situation which gave rise to this hymn. A man who was seriously ill, at death's door, has been cured; and this situation conjures up the experience of Israel who, after the agony of the exile, rediscovered the joy of praise. The people of Israel experienced their liberation as a kind of resurrection: "You restored me to life. . . ."

A SECOND READING: WITH JESUS

The church asks us to sing this psalm on a Sunday after Easter. What was only a metaphor for Israel became a wonderful reality for Jesus: "You have rescued me . . . you have raised my soul from the dead, restored me to life."

I like to imagine how Jesus must have felt in that first instant after his resurrection, as he came back from death to be restored to life. This is how Peter summed it up: "In the body he was put to death, in the *Spirit* he was raised to life" (1 P 3:18). And Paul said the same thing: "The first man, Adam . . . became a living soul; and the last Adam has become a *life-giving Spirit*" (1 Co 15:45). He later adds: "This Lord is the *Spirit,* and where the Spirit of the Lord is, there is *freedom*" (2 Co 3:17). But this is the most striking formula of them all: "What is sown is perishable, but what is raised is imperishable; what is sown is contemptible, but what is raised is glorious; what is sown is weak, but what is raised is powerful; what is sown is a natural body, but what is raised is a *spiritual body*" (1 Co 15:42–44). We can surmise from these mind-boggling scriptures that the resurrection of Jesus was much more than just biological resuscitation. Jesus was not merely restored to his former "limited" life: a life locked up within a particular nation, submissive to the laws of a particular race, and reduced to interaction with his close brothers and sisters. But he became the "Lord of Glory," the "Life-giving Spirit" for all times and places, for all cultures and all races.

A THIRD READING: WITH OUR TIME

1. *The Paschal Mystery* is the heart of our Christian faith, but if Christians are only people who believe in God, we are not different from the members of practically all the great religions. The distinguishing mark of our Christian faith is that we believe in Jesus Christ who died and is risen from the dead. Christian faith is much more than a complex set of doctrines or even a perfected moral code. *It is the meaning given to our existence* by the person of Jesus Christ.

We all know how wounded and sick our human nature is—when things go well, when our health is good we, like the psalmist, are tempted to delude ourselves and to say: "Nothing will ever disturb me!" We then incur the risk of moving away from God as we think: "I don't need Him! I can manage with my own strength!" Yet when God seems to veil his face, we are lost, for we are nothing without God. But we believe in the resurrection, we believe that God sent his son to heal men and women wounded by sin, we believe that our finitude is not meaningless, but that it opens unto the very *Spirit* of God, we believe that our death will be changed into life, we believe that our mourning and our decrepitude will be changed into dancing! Such is the *meaning* of our human existence. We are not on the way *toward* death, but *toward* the plenitude of life in God!

2. *"At Night There Are Tears, But Joy Comes with Dawn."* —What a remarkable poetic formula to describe the existential attitude of Christian men and women! We must be realistic and boldly face the evil of the world and our own evil, our sin. We must also be optimistic, never become discouraged but start anew every morning.

The "evening tears" are those precious tears that flow when we look back at our day and become aware of our failures and the ugliness of our sins, realizing all the burdens that have been added upon the human condition by the world around us. This "life evaluation" must be, above all, a realistic evaluation. Wise are the people who can honestly examine their day and responsibly judge their actions without any excessive guilt but also without any false pretense!

These evening tears are the prelude to happy mornings and new days of work and love, of courage and service. When we pass judgment on ourselves without any deceit we can then start anew and with shouts of joy—this is what Easter is all about!

PSALM 32

אַשְׁרֵי נְשׂוּי־פֶּשַׁע

YOU HAVE FORGIVEN MY SIN

1 Happy the man whose offence is forgiven,
  whose sin is remitted.
2 O happy the man to whom the Lord
  imputes no guilt,
  in whose spirit is no guile.

3 I kept it secret and my frame was wasted.
  I groaned all day long
4 for night and day your hand
  was heavy upon me.
  Indeed, my strength was dried up
  as by summer's heat.

5 But now I have acknowledged my sins;
  my guilt I did not hide.
  I said: "I will confess
  my offence to the Lord."
  And you, Lord, have forgiven
  the guilt of my sin.

6 So let every good man pray to you
  in the time of need.
  The floods of water may reach high
  but him they shall not reach.
7 You are my hiding place, O Lord;
  you save me from distress.
  (you surround me with cries of deliverance.)

*   *   *

8 I will instruct you and teach you
  the way you should go;

70

I will give you counsel
with my eye upon you.

9 Be not like horse and mule, unintelligent,
needing bridle and bit,
else they will not approach you.
10 Many sorrows has the wicked
but he who trusts in the Lord,
loving mercy surrounds him.

* * *

11 Rejoice, rejoice in the Lord,
exult, you just!
O come, ring out your joy,
all you upright of heart.

■

Happiness of the Forgiven Sinner

ACCOUNT OF THE EVENTS:
—before acknowledging my sins, I was filled with remorse,
—but I confessed my sins to God,
—and I found peace.

LESSONS OF WISDOM:
Pray in the time of need . . .
Seek refuge in God . . .
Do not be obstinate . . .
Trust in God's love . . .

A PRAYER OF THANKSGIVING:
Joy!
Exultation!

■

A FIRST READING: WITH ISRAEL

This psalm, attributed to David, is a forgiven sinner's prayer. Let us notice its marvelous boldness. Instead of hiding in the secrecy of his private conscience, this guilty man confesses in public that he is a sinner and uses his own experience of forgiveness to draw lessons of wisdom that can be useful to all. At the conclusion of the psalm he invites everybody to celebrate with joy and exultation the forgiveness he has received.

Let us also notice the purity of this religious attitude. The tragedy of sin is found within our relationship with God, and what matters most is not the psychological phenomenon of remorse and shame, but the breaking of the Covenant, followed by renewed dialogue between two people who loved each other, hurt each other, and forgave each other.

"Happy the man whose offence is forgiven . . . I acknowledged my sins . . . and you, Lord, have forgiven (me) . . . you are my hiding place . . . he who trusts in the Lord, *loving mercy* surrounds him . . ." We have here the key words of the Covenant: *"loving mercy."*

A SECOND READING: WITH JESUS

We are irresistibly reminded of the three parables of God's mercy which, like this psalm, all end with the same refrain: "Rejoice with me . . . I tell you, there will be . . . rejoicing in heaven over one repentant sinner" (Lk 15:6, 9, 32).

For Jesus also, the forgiveness of sins was a matter of love. To Simon the Pharisee, who was priding himself on his haughty moral integrity, Jesus gave the model of the wretched woman who was a sinner but publicly bewailed her sins. He said to him: "I tell you that her sins, many as they are, have been forgiven her, because she has shown such great love. It is someone who is forgiven little who shows little love" (Lk 7:47–50).

A THIRD READING: WITH OUR TIME

1. *Interaction of Mind and Body*—Studies in biology and psychology have revealed the profound unity of the human being:

the mind affects the body and the body influences the spirit. The semitic mentality even went one step further when it stated that sin could actually cause disease: "I kept (my sin) secret and my frame was wasted. I groaned all day long for night and day your hand was heavy upon me. Indeed, my strength was dried up as by summer's heat." Jesus reacted against this too rigorous idea of a connection between sin and corporal punishment: "Neither he nor his parents sinned that he should have been born blind" (Jn 9:3). It is true, nevertheless, that sin is unhealthy, and Freud initiated a therapeutic method whose main tenet is the recognition and acknowledgement of whatever is hidden in the deepest recesses of our psyche.

2. *Acknowledgement; The Source of Liberation*—"You surround me with cries of deliverance," said the sinner who acknowledged his sins, stressing the profound freedom which resulted from this process: "Be not like horse and mule, unintelligent, needing bridle and bit." When we truly acknowledge our sin we become free, and we no longer need "bridle and bit." We take responsibility for our actions and we act on our own.

3. *Acknowledgement; An Act of Truth*—Human beings degrade themselves to the utmost when they try to justify the evil they commit by calling "white" what is "black." To confess one's sins is not degrading; rather it is an act of truth, it is noble. No lie is worse than the lie we tell ourselves when we try to disguise evil as good. The psalmist said: "Happy the man in whose spirit is no guile," and Jesus told us: "Whoever does the truth comes out into the light" (Jn 3:21), and "The truth will set you free" (Jn 8:32).

4. *The Sacrament of Reconciliation As A Celebration*—The sin which we hide within us literally poisons our conscience, like a hidden corpse. We can therefore understand why reconciliation is becoming more of a joyous celebration.

"Rejoice, rejoice in the Lord, exult, you just! O come, ring out your joy, all you upright of heart!"

PSALM 33

רַנְּנוּ צַדִּיקִים בַּיהוָה

HAPPY THE PEOPLE WHOSE GOD IS THE LORD!

1   Ring out your joy to the Lord, O you just;
for praise is fitting for loyal hearts.

2   Give thanks to the Lord upon the harp,
with a ten-stringed lute sing him songs.
3   O sing him a song that is new,
play loudly, with all your skill.

4   For the word of the Lord is faithful
and all his works to be trusted.
5   The Lord loves justice and right
and fills the earth with his love.

6   By his word the heavens were made,
by the breath of his mouth all the stars.
7   He collects the waves of the ocean;
he stores up the depths of the sea.

8   Let all the earth fear the Lord,
all who live in the world revere him.
9   He spoke; and it came to be.
He commanded; it sprang into being.

10 He frustrates the designs of nations,
he defeats the plans of the peoples.
11 His own designs shall stand for ever,
the plans of his heart from age to age.

12 They are happy, whose God is the Lord,
the people he has chosen as his own.
13 From the heavens the Lord looks forth,
he sees all the children of men.

14 From the place where he dwells he gazes
   on all the dwellers on the earth,
15 he who shapes the hearts of them all
   and considers all their deeds.

16 A king is not saved by his army,
   nor a warrior preserved by his strength.
17 A vain hope for safety is the horse;
   despite its power it cannot save.

18 The Lord looks on those who revere him,
   on those who hope in his love,
19 to rescue their souls from death,
   to keep them alive in famine.

20 Our soul is waiting for the Lord.
   The Lord is our help and our shield.
21 In him do our hearts find joy.
   We trust his holy name.

22 May your love be upon us, O Lord,
   as we place all our hope in you.

■

AN INVITATION TO PRAISE
   —ring out your joy . . .
   —give thanks . . .
   —play musical instruments . . .
   —sing . . .
   —praise with all your strength . . .

**TO THE GOD OF CREATION, SOVEREIGN MASTER OF
THE COSMOS**
   —the earth . . .
      he loved it into being
      with his creative Word
      with his Breath which is Spirit

—the sea . . .
    everything obeys him.

TO THE GOD OF PROVIDENCE, SOVEREIGN MASTER OF HISTORY
    A God who "intervenes . . ."
    —who overthrows evil designs . . .
    —who has a plan which *he* is in the process of fulfilling,
    —through the "mediation" of his chosen people
    —without neglecting any inhabitant of the earth!
        all have been created by him . . .
        all are known to him . . .

TO THE GOD OF SALVATION
    —salvation cannot be found in anything "human"
    —the only salvation is in God . . . because he loves us so
        much that he saves us from death!
    . . . total dependency
    . . . help, protection
    . . . joy, trust.

CONCLUSION:
    In response to so much Love,
    invincible hope!

■

A FIRST READING: WITH ISRAEL

Hebrew poetry makes frequent use of parallelism. Verses go two by two, and the second one echoes the idea of the first one, for example:

1. "He frustrates *the designs of nations*
2. he defeats *the plans of the peoples*."
1. "By *his word the heavens* were made
   By *the breath* of his mouth *all the stars*."

A SECOND READING: WITH JESUS

Jesus is the word, the creative word, and "through him all things came into being" (Jn 1:3).

He gives us light and life and permeates every one of our actions (Jn 1:9).

He gave thanks to the Father for his redemptive love (The Last Supper, the eucharist).

He tells us: "the Father himself loves you" (Jn 16:27). The earth is filled with his love . . . the designs of his *heart* stand from age to age . . . Here is this heart who so loved the world!"

The Lord is watching to "preserve our souls from death." Only Jesus' resurrection truly fulfills God's plan, the design of the heart of God. Happy are they who choose God as their Lord! The Beatitudes . . .

A THIRD READING: WITH OUR TIME

We have to personalize this psalm in our own style and in our own lives: We must *praise,* we must *believe* in the power of God . . . believe that today God still intervenes in contemporary events. . . . We must "become poor."

"The Lord looks on those who revere him" and the watchful eye of God is a better protection than any human power.

Let us therefore shout our joy to the Lord!

PSALM 34

אֲבָרֲכָה אֶת־יְהוָה

TASTE AND SEE THAT THE LORD IS GOOD!

2 I will bless the Lord at all times,
   his praise always on my lips;
3 in the Lord my soul shall make its boast.
   The humble shall hear and be glad.

4 Glorify the Lord with me.
   Together let us praise his name.
5 I sought the Lord and he answered me;
   from all my terrors he set me free.

6 Look towards him and be radiant;
   let your faces not be abashed.
7 This poor man called; the Lord heard him
   and rescued him from all his distress.

8 The angel of the Lord is encamped
   around those who revere him, to rescue them.
9 Taste and see that the Lord is good.
   He is happy who seeks refuge in him.

10 Revere the Lord, you his saints.
    They lack nothing, those who revere him.
11 Strong lions suffer want and go hungry
    but those who seek the Lord lack no blessing.

12 Come, children, and hear me
    that I might teach you the fear of the Lord.
13 Who is he who longs for life
    and many days, to enjoy his prosperity?

14 Then keep your tongue from evil
    and your lips from speaking deceit.

15 Turn aside from evil and do good;
   seek and strive after peace.

16 The Lord turns his face against the wicked
   to destroy their remembrance from the earth.
17 The Lord turns his eyes to the just
   and his ears to their appeal.

18 They call and the Lord hears
   and rescues them in all their distress.
19 The Lord is close to the broken-hearted;
   those whose spirit is crushed he will save.

20 Many are the trials of the just man
   but from them all the Lord will rescue him.
21 He will keep guard over all his bones,
   not one of his bones shall be broken.

22 Evil brings death to the wicked;
   those who hate the good are doomed.
23 The lord ransoms the souls of his servants.
   Those who hide in him shall not be condemned.

■

AN INVITATION TO GIVE THANKS:
   Bless the Lord . . .
   Praise him . . .
   Glorify him . . .
   Magnify him . . .
   Exalt him . . .

REASONS FOR THIS PRAYER
   God answers us
   God delivers us
   God hears us
   God saves us
   God watches over us

EXHORTATIONS: THE WAY TO HAPPINESS
Adore . . .
Listen . . .
Keep away from evil . . .
Do good . . .
Seek peace . . .

God watches . . .
God listens attentively . . .
God turns against the wicked . . .

God hears us . . .
God delivers us . . .
God is close to the broken-hearted . . .
God saves us . . .

God keeps watch over us . . .

■

A FIRST READING: WITH ISRAEL

This is an alphabetical psalm in which each verse starts with a letter of the Hebrew alphabet. Of whom is this psalm talking? Who is invited to give thanks? They are the poor, the *anawim*. "The humble shall hear and be glad." They who are unhappy, poor, humble; they whose hearts are bleeding, they are said to be happy whereas the rich are said to be destitute!

A SECOND READING: WITH JESUS

"How blessed are the poor in spirit: the kingdom of Heaven is theirs" (Mt 5:3). Thanks to psalms like this one, we are better able to understand how much Jesus was "impregnated" with the prayers of his people . . . just like Mary, whose "Magnificat" we rediscover here.

The soul of Jesus was always in an atmosphere of praise and thanksgiving, and one of his prayers reminds us of the tenor of this psalm: "I bless you Father, Lord of heaven and of earth, for hiding these things from the learned and the clever and revealing them to little children" (Lk 10:21).

The fourth evangelist explicitly quoted this psalm when he explained why the soldier pierced the side of the crucified Jesus instead of breaking his legs, as he had just done to the other two crucified men: "Instead of breaking his legs one of the soldiers pierced his side with a lance . . . all this happened to fulfil the words of scripture: 'not one bone of his will be broken' " (Jn 19:34–36; Ps 34:21).

Let us listen to this paradox: Jesus who was the Poor in the highest sense of the word, invited us to listen to his prayer of thanksgiving because the Lord watched over him and did not permit any of his bones to be broken! We can see once more that the Bible urges us to a deeper reading and how this promise of happiness cannot be understood in the literal and materialistic sense. What this means is that we must think of Jesus when we hear the psalmist tell us: "Many are the trials of the just man, but from them all the Lord will rescue him. He will keep guard over all his bones, not one of his bones shall be broken." Only the resurrection can ultimately fulfil this promise.

A THIRD READING: WITH OUR TIME

1. *"This Poor Man Called: The Lord Heard Him"*—A strong current is now running through our society. We want to be more attentive to the poor, we would like to achieve greater social equality, and we are trying to help the underprivileged with all kinds of laws. This new awareness is a sign of hope, but if we refuse to listen to the "cry of the poor," we clearly exclude ourselves from the plan of God.

"A poor person calls, God is listening!" When we say this we are sometimes accused of dabbling in politics, but this accusation is made in total ignorance of the religious message of the gospel and if we refuse to take the side of the poor against social inequalities and injustices we cannot possibly call ourselves "religious." We must take a stand; there is no choice possible! We do, however, have a rightful choice as far as options are concerned, and our opinions may differ on the concrete means of achieving this goal. Let us not forget that, in regard to burning social issues, the true problem lies not within our western economic systems as such, but in the disparity they create between industrialized nations which have conquered hunger and Third World countries whose people are dying of hunger!

Let us reread psalm 34 from this point of view.

2. *An Invitation to Action: To Liberate, to Save, to Abolish Evil*—"The humble shall hear and be glad . . ." How can we possibly say this verse—without being hypocrites—unless we engage all of our energies in the struggle to make it happen?

3. *The Assurance of Happiness*—If we want to be happy we must "turn aside from evil and do good." We must seek God and adore him. "How naive!" the free-thinker will say. . . . But what if it were true? What if the only people to be truly happy were the ones the psalmist tells us about? Let us give it a try!

PSALM 40

קַוֹּה קִוִּיתִי יְהֹוָה

HERE I AM, LORD

2 I waited, I waited for the Lord
and he stooped down to me;
he heard my cry.

3 He drew me from the deadly pit,
from the miry clay.
He set my feet upon a rock
and made my footsteps firm.

4 He put a new song into my mouth,
praise of our God.
Many shall see and fear
and shall trust in the Lord.

5 Happy the man who has placed
his trust in the Lord
and has not gone over to the rebels
who follow false gods.

6 How many, O Lord my God,
are the wonders and designs
that you have worked for us;
you have no equal.
Should I proclaim and speak of them,
they are more than I can tell!

7 You do not ask for sacrifice and offerings,
but an open ear.
You do not ask for holocaust and victim.
8 Instead, here I am.

In the scroll of the book stands written

 9 that I should do your will.
My God, I delight in your law
in the depth of my heart.

10 Your justice I have proclaimed
in the great assembly.
My lips I have not sealed;
you know it, O Lord.

11 I have not hidden your justice in my heart
but declared your faithful help.
I have not hidden your love and your truth
from the great assembly.

12 O Lord, you will not withhold
your compassion from me.
Your merciful love and your truth
will always guard me.

13 For I am beset with evils
too many to be counted.
My sins have fallen upon me
and my sight fails me.
They are more than the hairs of my head
and my heart sinks.

14 O Lord, come to my rescue,
Lord, come to my aid.
15 O let there be shame and confusion
on those who seek my life.

O let them turn back in confusion,
who delight in my harm
16 Let them be appalled, covered with shame,
who jeer at my lot.

17 O let there be rejoicing and gladness
for all who seek you.
Let them ever say: "The Lord is great,"
who love your saving help.

18 As for me, wretched and poor,
    the Lord thinks of me.
    You are my rescuer, my help,
    O God, do not delay.

■

MY SITUATION:
    —I was in pain . . .
    —I waited . . .
    —I cried out to God . . .
    —He saved me . . .
    —I give thanks to him . . .

MY PRAYER OF THANKSGIVING:
    —I must be proud of my faith . . .
    —I must stand in awe of You, Lord . . .
    —I must not offer merely "ritual" sacrifices . . .
    —I must do your will . . .
      in the heart of my daily life . . .
    —I must proclaim the Good News to all . . .
        your justice,
        your salvation,
        your *love,*
        your *truth.*

MY RENEWED APPEAL:
    —I am still in pain, Lord!
    —I am still a sinner!
    —Come to my rescue!
      Help me!
    —Let all who want to hurt me turn back!
    —Let there be Joy for all who seek *you,* O Lord!
    —I am wretched and "poor," but *you* are thinking of me,
      you will rescue me . . . Do not delay!

■

A FIRST READING: WITH ISRAEL

The movement of this psalm of thanksgiving is remarkable: first a plea in the midst of a dramatic situation, then thanksgiving after the prayer has been granted; but it is not over yet, and there is a renewed supplication in the midst of new evils.

A few marvelous metaphors:

"I was in a deadly pit . . . he stooped down to me; he heard my cry . . . he set my feet upon a rock and made my footsteps firm . . . he put a new song into my mouth . . . I delight in your law in the depth of my heart . . . My lips I have not sealed . . . My sins have fallen upon me and my sight fails me . . . My heart sinks."

There is something amazing and mysterious about this situation: the supplicant, surrounded by a great crowd, has come to the temple to offer a ritual sacrifice . . . but "Where is the victim?" they ask. The answer is unprecedented: God no longer wants sacrifices of animals . . . what God wants is "an open ear," submissiveness to *his will* . . . God wants us to give ourselves— out of love!

A SECOND READING: WITH JESUS

In the Letter to the Hebrews, Paul used the very words of this psalm to meditate on the sacrificial offering Jesus made of himself: He said, on coming into the world: "You wanted no sacrifice or cereal offering, but you gave me a body. You took no pleasure in burnt offering or sacrifice for sin; then I said, 'HERE I AM, I am coming,' in the scroll of the book (in Psalm 40) it is written of me, *to do your will, God*" (Heb 10:5–10).

Thus a scripture inspired by God shows us that Jesus was saying this psalm with enthusiasm and that he found in it one of the clearest expressions of his permanent "gift of self" to the Father and to his brothers and sisters, until the time of the "total gift" of himself on the cross.

Jesus also said: "My food is to do the *will* of the one who sent me . . . (Jn 4:34). And he echoed this psalm at the very hour he decided to offer himself in sacrifice: "My Father, if it is possible, let this cup pass me by. Nevertheless, let it be as *you*, not I would have it" (Mt 26:39).

A THIRD READING: WITH OUR TIME

As we have seen, this psalm is, first and foremost, the prayer of Jesus. It is also *our* prayer, but we must take care not to succumb to ritualism. God does not want from us external sacrifices or external prayers; what he wants is our flesh and blood, the gift of our daily life, our spiritual sacrifice. (1 P 2:5; Rm 12:1).

We can expand on the central assertion of this psalm and say that God expects us to offer our daily actions rather than just our Sunday prayers. My "thanks-giving" (my eucharist) should be: to be proud of my faith, to stand in awe of God, to live according to his will, and to proclaim the gospel: the good news of his justice and his salvation, of his love and his truth.

One way of rereading this psalm would be to follow the development of the prayer as it unfolds while applying the suggestions given to our daily life.

"Here I am, O Lord . . . to do your will."

PSALM 47

כָּל־הָעַמִּים תִּקְעוּ־כָף

GOD REIGNS OVER ALL

2 All peoples, clap your hands,
   cry to God with shouts of joy!
3 For the Lord, the Most High, we must fear,
   great king over all the earth.

4 He subdues peoples under us
   and nations under our feet.
5 Our inheritance, our glory, is from him,
   given to Jacob out of love.

6 God goes up with shouts of joy;
   the Lord goes up with trumpet blast.
7 Sing praise for God, sing praise,
   sing praise to our king, sing praise.

8 God is king of all the earth,
   Sing praise with all your skill.
9 God is king over the nations;
   God reigns on his holy throne.

10 The princes of the people are assembled
    with the people of Abraham's God.
    The rulers of the earth belong to God,
    to God who reigns over all.

■

ALL PEOPLE . . .
   Clap your hands, shout with Joy,
      "God is King!"

CHOSEN PEOPLE:
    People of Jacob
      "God goes up!"

      Sing praise, sing praise,
      sing praise, sing praise,
      SING!

    People of Abraham

■

A FIRST READING: WITH ISRAEL

On one of the days of the Festival of Tabernacles Jerusalem would celebrate God, her *king*. The procession would start from the spring of Gihon, in the heart of the Kidron valley, and then would ascend the mountain of Zion where the temple stood. In a kind of symbolic reenactment, the congregation would enthrone God. And God was indeed present to the rejoicing of his people. Of course, this celebration did not "give" kingship to Yahweh who has been king for ever . . . but it actualized this kingship. By virtue of this celebration, God was in effect ruling —in a more concrete way—over this people who acknowledged him as king.

As in every royal ideology, God was perceived as a great king, the Most High, reigning on his holy throne, subduing all his enemies, and receiving homage from "the princes of the people." The accession of the King to his throne took place amidst the exuberant acclamations of the people, and the doorjambs of the temple must indeed have shaken under the thundering "Holy, holy" as Isaiah reported.

How bold was this small nation which practically never had any political or military power compared with Egypt and Babylon, its powerful neighbors! How bold the people were to think and dare to say that their king, their God was "King of all the earth!" How bold they were to shout that their king was victorious when the whole history of Israel shows us a nation occupied and subdued by neighbors who constantly pillaged it!

A SECOND READING: WITH JESUS

This was a prophetic vision, and what was never fulfilled on a human level became a mysterious reality in Jesus Christ. The phrase "God goes up," which is at the heart of this psalm, was awaiting its fulfilment. From the beginning, the church used this phrase and applied it to the *ascension* of the risen Christ in the glory of the Father. But beyond this phrase, it is truly the universal kingship of God which is sung in this psalm and which the feast of the Ascension celebrates. Jesus was humiliated for a while, "he emptied himself, taking the form of a slave" (Ph 2:7), but on Easter Day, "God raised him high, and gave him the name which is above all other names" (Ph 2:9). This is when he took possession of his kingdom where "he is seated at the right hand of God and worshipped by all the celestial beings" . . . having already conquered his enemies in a symbolical manner and awaiting the day when he "will hand over the kingdom to God the Father, having abolished every principality, every ruling force and power" (1 Co 15:24).

A THIRD READING: WITH OUR TIME

1. *Ascension: Joy of Humankind That Sees Itself "Crowned" in One of Its Own*—A man, a member of our own mortal race who accepted his human condition unto death, is enjoying the plenitude of the *glory of God* now and for ever. And scripture tells us that some day this man will bestow the same glory on us, for he is "the first-born" of the entire creation and what happened to him will also happen to us.

When we are tempted to despair, we should ponder on this mystery of uplifting, of ascension, for this is where the eminent dignity of the human race finds its deepest justification. There is a king hidden in the poorest of the poor. The human wretch, the broken man, the woman bespattered with blemishes, are destined for the "royal and divine condition." What will I do to promote the dignity and improve the living conditions of my fellow human beings?

2. *Elected People . . . Chosen People . . . Peoples of the Earth . . . All the Peoples . . .*—We notice in this psalm the dialectics between a "particularistic" pole (the conviction of being the chosen people, beloved by God) and a "universalistic" pole (a call to all people to adore the true God). We cannot possibly limit ourselves to the image of a submission which would be imposed upon us by force: "shouts of joy" cannot be uttered by conquered people and the clapping of hands is definitely not a gesture of submission. In spite of the vocabulary, which could be misleading, ("he subdues peoples under us") we have here a freely chosen gathering, a feast. Heaven is not a dictatorship or a forced-labor camp, but a gigantic festive celebration. And the kingdom of Jesus Christ has little in common with earthly king-

doms where "their rulers lord it over them . . . Among you this is not to happen" (Mk 10:42).

3. *Shouts of Joy . . . Hand-Clappings*—We must joyfully participate in this acclamation to God, and the liturgy often invites us to do so; unfortunately, we remain terribly cold and mute.

We must also invite others to be part of this celebration for God and extend to them, not a reluctant invitation in the hope that they will be converted, but a joyful, heartfelt invitation to share in the joy of the children of the King. Come to the wedding feast! (Mk 2:19; Lk 14:17).

4. *God, the Great King, the Most High, the Almighty*—Some day, on the Last Day, we shall be dazzled by divine grandeur, but for now God is amazingly discreet and invisible. But nothing prevents us from anticipating that Day . . . right now!

PSALM 51

הָנֵּנִי אֱלֹהִים כְּחַסְדֶּךָ

RENEW MY SPIRIT, O LORD!

3   Have mercy on me, God, in your love.*
    In your compassion blot out my offence.
4   O wash me more and more from my guilt
    and cleanse me from my sin.

5   My offenses truly I know them;
    my sin is always before me.
6   Against you, you alone, have I sinned;
    what is evil in your sight I have done.

    That you may be justified when you give sentence
    and be without reproach when you judge
7   O see, in guilt I was born,
    a sinner was I conceived.

8   Indeed you love truth in the heart;
    then in the secret of my heart teach me wisdom
9   O purify me, then I shall be clean;
    O wash me, I shall be whiter than snow.

10 Make me hear rejoicing and gladness,
    that the bones you have crushed may dance.†
11 From my sins turn away your face
    and blot out all my guilt.

12 A pure heart create for me, O God,
    put a steadfast spirit within me.

---

* For v. 3 the Grail version reads "kindness" instead of "love."
† For v. 10 the Grail version reads "thrill" instead of "dance."

13   Do not cast me away from your presence,
     nor deprive me of your holy spirit.

14   Give me again the joy of your help;
     with a spirit of fervour sustain me,
15   that I may teach transgressors your ways
     and sinners may return to you.

16   O rescue me, God, my helper,
     and my tongue shall ring out your goodness.
17   O Lord, open my lips
     and my mouth shall declare your praise.

18   For in sacrifice you take no delight,
     burnt offering from me you would refuse,
19   my sacrifice, a contrite spirit.
     A humbled, contrite heart you will not spurn.

20   In your goodness, show favour to Zion:
     rebuild the walls of Jerusalem.
21   Then you will be pleased with lawful sacrifice,
     (burnt offerings wholly consumed),
     then you will be offered young bulls on your altar.

■

A Psalm of Repentance: The Prayer of a Sinner Asking for Forgiveness

CONFESSING HIS SINS:
   I know my sin
   I have done what is evil

   Evil has been deeply rooted within me
   even before I was born!

ASKING FOR FORGIVENESS:
   Purify me
   Wash me

Give back to me my rejoicing
                    my dancing

Remove my guilt

Re-create me
Renew me

Give me joy again

A PROMISE OF THANKSGIVING:
I will be an apostle
I will worship you
I will praise you
I will change my life
I will offer a sacrifice of thanksgiving

■

A FIRST READING: WITH ISRAEL

This psalm is said to have been composed by David after he had Uriah murdered in order to take his wife Bathsheba. The king's sin, as well as his admirable contrition, have remained a symbol of sin and forgiveness. But in the background we also have the tragic destruction of Jerusalem and the ensuing deportation of the people to Babylon: sin as well as repentance have collective repercussions. (". . . rebuild the walls of Jerusalem.")

The cry of repentance is expressed here with an admirable simplicity: This sinner is unhappy *only* because of his sin, and his sin is nothing but an offence against God. There is nothing fundamentally morbid in this attitude, and Israel had a very positive idea about sin. The sinner is not left alone with his remorse but he is "before somebody" who loves him. Everything flows from love.

A SECOND READING WITH JESUS

When Jesus wanted to explain the wonder of God's pardon, he invented the parable of the "Father of the Prodigal Son," in which he spontaneously used expressions from Psalm 51: "Against you, you alone, have I sinned." He also conveyed the joy of forgiveness with "singing and dancing," just like the psalmist.

When Jesus instituted the sacrament of baptism for the remission of sins, he used the same great symbol of purification: "O wash me, I shall be whiter than snow."

When he forgave Mary of Magdala, the woman who was a sinner, he also made an apostle of her, so that she "may teach transgressors (God's) ways."* It is she—a former prostitute—who was the first witness of the resurrection and who was commissioned by Jesus: "Go and find my brothers . . ." (Jn 20:17). And after the Holy Spirit re-created the disciples with his Breath on Pentecost, their tongues were loosened and they sang the Lord's praises.

---

* Translator's note: Most New Testament scholars no longer identify Mary of Magdala with the "sinful woman."

Finally, Jesus gave his approval to the scribe who, in the line of this psalm, stated that to love God and one's neighbor was "far more important than any burnt offering or sacrifice" (Mk 12:33).

A THIRD READING: WITH OUR TIME

1. *The Deep Roots of Evil*—Modern psychology has emphasized how strongly influenced we are by heredity, physical conditioning and social influences. Even in his day the psalmist felt the burden of this determinism, and although he was very much aware of the evil he had done, he felt incapable of redressing his wrong, no matter how strong his desire was. He must therefore ask for God's help . . . He knew the root of sin to be within his human condition, even prior to any personal culpability: "In guilt I was born, a sinner was I conceived."

2. *Yet, This Attitude Is Not Fatalistic*—"My offences truly I know them . . . what is evil in your sight I have done." This person took responsibility for his own actions and did not try in any way to justify his conduct. Self-justification is too often a denial of personal responsibility. Help us, O Lord, to see clearly within ourselves and to become aware of the evil we perpetrate.

3. *The True Meaning of Sin*—We water down the reality of sin when we talk about "transgressions" or "faults." David did know that in killing Uriah and seducing his wife he had committed more than a "mistake" or a "blunder." He knew he had committed a *sin,* a sin against *God:* "against *you,* you alone, have I sinned." Sin has to be judged in relation to a transcendent God and it must be measured against love, for it is a breach of love. When I sin I reject the love of the One who loves me.

4. *The True Meaning of Forgiveness*—Consequently, forgiveness is also a matter of love. "Have mercy on me, God, in your *love.* In your compassion blot out my offence." Forgiveness means renewal. The poet uses a rich vocabulary to put this renewal into words and he even refers to it as a "new creation." Forgiving does not mean only forgetting the past or "deep-cleansing" the soul, it means bringing forth a "new being." What a touching mystery, retold a thousand times throughout the Bible! There is nothing morbid or obsessive about sin ac-

cording to God. Sin can actually lead to indescribable joy and to thanksgiving.

5. *Collective Solidarity*—Sin is an eminently personal reality, yet the Bible unceasingly tells us that it also has repercussions reaching far beyond the sinner. This is what modern sociologists call "collective responsibility." Each one of our sins weighs upon our brothers and sisters, and every effort we make to turn away from sin contributes to the betterment of the quality of their lives. The psalmist already knew that his sin and his repentance affected his fellow human beings and as he was "converted" he pledged to help them: ". . . that I may teach transgressors your ways and sinners may return to you." In addition he associates the reconstruction of the city to the reconstruction of his own being: "In your goodness, show favor to Zion: rebuild the walls of Jerusalem." The church of today has been trying to restore this sense of community to the sacrament of reconciliation, and there is much truth in the old adage: "The soul that lifts itself up lifts the world up."

6. *The True Repentance That Pleases God*—God is not the primary winner when we come to recognize our evil: sin is a form of self-destruction and a principle of death. What concerns God, according to this psalm, is that we stop destroying ourselves and that we receive a new heart and a new life. Then, when harmony and beauty have been restored in our lives, we will be truly happy and able to sing God's praises.

PSALM 63

אֱלֹהִים אֵלִי אַתָּה

FOR YOU I LONG, O LORD

2   O God, you are my God, for you I long
    (as soon as the day breaks)*
    for you my soul is thirsting.
    My body pines for you
    like a dry, weary land without water.
3   So I gaze on you in the sanctuary
    to see your strength and your glory.

4   For your love is better than life,
    my lips will speak your praise.
5   So I will bless you all my life,
    in your name I will lift up my hands.
6   My soul shall be filled as with a banquet,
    my mouth shall praise you with joy.

7   In the watches of the night I remember you
    I spend hours talking to you†
8   for you have been my help;
    in the shadow of your wings I rejoice.
9   My soul clings to you;
    your right hand holds me fast.

10   Those who seek to destroy my life
    shall go down to the depths of the earth.
11   They shall be put into the power of the sword
    and left as the prey of the jackals.

---

* Not in the Grail version.
† For v 7 the Grail version reads:
  "On my bed I remember you.
  On you I muse through the night."

99

12   But the king shall rejoice in God;
      (all that swear by him shall be blessed)
      for the mouth of liars shall be silenced.

■

Burning Desire for the Presence of God

MY SOUL IS THIRSTING FOR YOU!
    —image of the parched earth of the Middle East waiting
      for rain

TO BE WITH YOU IS THE HAPPINESS I LONG FOR!
    —image of the banquet which satiates
    —image of the song which makes the heart glad
    —image of the little bird that cheeps with joy under its
      mother's wings.
    —image of the bride cradled in the bridegroom's arms

THIS HAPPINESS IS NOT EASY TO OBTAIN AND IT
MUST BE CONQUERED FROM THE POWERS OF EVIL

   *But We Are Confident of Happiness for God Will Triumph
   In the End.*

■

A FIRST READING: WITH ISRAEL

The first four stanzas sing the joy of the "Guest of Yahweh," who likes to visit God in his house, his temple, and who even likes to dwell there, like a Levite. They sing the joy of communion with God, the joy of intimate prayer. Let us notice the unusual, affectionate, use of the second-person pronouns (seventeen of them!): "*you* are my God, for *you* I long, for *you* my soul is thirsting, *your* strength, *your* glory, *your* love, *your* name." Adopting the same linguistic device and interiorizing these pronouns could be one way of praying this psalm: "*You* are here, Lord, I am speaking to *you,* listen to me."

The last two stanzas are quite different (the poet no longer uses the second person), and they are the evocation of the eschatological battle which will eradicate evil from the earth. Some exegetes feel that they were not part of the original psalm, and they certainly can shock someone who has not been forewarned of their deeper meaning, as the violence expressed here is contrary to our present-day mentality of tolerance and nonsectarianism. But, as a matter of fact, most of the Psalms of Communion with God have a similar stanza directed against the enemies of God. This attitude is, after all, understandable: true love for somebody demands the disappearance of the people who hurt the one we love. It also stresses the fact that happiness in the presence of God is not to be understood as a flight from reality or an indolent evasion, but rather as an added invitation to total commitment to a daily fight against evil. For Israel, prayer was never cut off from life.

From a literary standpoint, let us savor the picturesque quality of the images that dot the poem: the thirsty soul, the "weary land without water," the banquet, the little bird hiding "in the shadow of (his mother's) wings," the hand that "holds fast," "Your *love* is better than life." We have here the keyword of the Covenant: your love, your *hesed.*

A SECOND READING: WITH JESUS

We can easily put this psalm in Jesus' mouth:
"In the Watches of the Night I Remember You, I Spend Hours

Talking to You"—Mark tells us that this is exactly what Jesus did: "In the morning, long before dawn, he got up and left the house and went off to a lonely place and prayed there" (Mk 1:35).

"*My Soul Shall Be Filled As with A Banquet*"—Jesus often used this very image to show that the messianic banquet was taking place: "Look, my banquet is all prepared . . ." (Mt 22:4). And it was Jesus who instituted the "meal" in which we share his bread and his cup of blessings: "Take and eat . . . take and drink!"

"*I Remember You*"—Jesus, too, invited us to remember him: "Do this in memory of me."

"*Your Right Hand Holds Me Fast*"—Jesus depicted this remarkable father who threw his arms around his son's neck and kissed him tenderly when he returned home. "The disciple Jesus loved was reclining next to Jesus" at the last Supper (Jn 13:23, 21:20).

"*Your Love Is Better Than Life*"—No one more than Jesus experienced the true communion with God about which this psalm sings. "I have loved you just as the Father has loved me" (Jn 15:9). It is therefore fitting that we should say this psalm with Jesus since he came down from heaven in order to usher us into the intimacy he himself shares with God.

"*They Shall Be Put into the Power of the Sword*"—No! This is where the similarity ends! Jesus did not say that. In fact, he said the exact opposite when his foes came to arrest him in the Garden of Olives and he told Peter: "Put your sword back!" (Mt 26:52) and later: "Forgive them; they do not know what they are doing" (Lk 23:34). If we want to say these last two stanzas of imprecation it is imperative that we transpose them to the eschatological level and that we ask God to eradicate evil. By doing so we will echo the prayer of Jesus: "Deliver us from evil."

"*I Gaze On you In the Sanctuary . . . I Spend Hours Talking to You*"—Jesus dared say that the true temple, the only place where the Divine Presence would reside from then on was his body. "I have power to destroy the temple of God and in three days build it up" (Mt 26:61). For this reason, praying this psalm in front of a tabernacle could not be more fitting!

A THIRD READING: WITH OUR TIME

Our time seems to be rediscovering *intimate prayer*. Psalm 63 is the prayer of a person who is well-versed in this form of prayer, but the attitudes he advocates seem so lofty to us, so intensely mystical . . . to the point that we may feel insincere if we try to adopt them ourselves. After all, who among us can honestly say to God: "I spend hours talking to you."? or "For you I long at daybreak . . . for you my soul is thirsting . . ."? Instead we often forget even our morning prayer and we succumb to indifference.

But it is precisely in the *materialistic context of our modern world* that we should keep praying these burning words of the psalm—which, we know, were inspired by God—and perhaps, little by little, the joy on our lips, our "raised hands," our shouts of joy will also cause the deepest recesses of our *hearts* to be transformed.

The expressions used in the psalm are all "bodily" expressions, and it is true that we should not despise our bodies. In fact, we must rediscover gestures and attitudes of the body that will facilitate prayer. Sometimes, when we are kneeling or bowed down in the presence of God, only our body is praying while our mind is wandering. And after all, communion with the Bread of Life is an eminently "bodily" gesture, an efficacious sign of intimacy with the presence of Christ which expresses a profound reality beyond the tangible and the rational.

PSALM 66 הָרִיעוּ לֵאלֹהִים כָּל־הָאָרֶץ

COME AND SEE THE WORKS OF GOD

1 Cry out with joy to the God all the earth,
2 O sing to the glory of his name.
  O render him glorious praise.
3 Say to God: "How tremendous your deeds!"

  Because of the greatness of your strength
  your enemies cringe before you.
4 Before you all the earth shall bow;
  shall sing to you, sing to your name!

5 Come and see the works of God,
  tremendous his deeds among men.
6 He turned the sea into dry land,
  they passed through the river dry-shod.

  Let our joy then be in him;
7 he rules for ever by his might.
  His eyes keep watch over the nations:
  let rebels not rise against him.

8 O peoples, bless our God,
  let the voice of his praise resound,
9 of the God who gave life to our souls
  and kept our feet from stumbling.

10 For you, O God, have tested us,
   you have tried us as silver is tried:
11 you led us, God, into the snare;
   you laid a heavy burden on our backs.

12 You let men ride over our heads;
   we went through fire and through water
   but then you brought us relief.

13 Burnt offering I bring to your house;
   to you I will pay my vows,
14 the vows which my lips have uttered,
   which my mouth spoke in my distress.

15 I will offer burnt offerings of fatlings
   with the smoke of burning rams.
   I will offer bullocks and goats.

16 Come and hear, all who fear God.
   I will tell what he did for my soul:
17 to him I cried aloud,
   with high praise ready on my tongue.

18 If there had been evil in my heart,
   the Lord would not have listened.
19 But truly God has listened;
   he has heeded the voice of my prayer.

20 Blessed be God who did not reject my prayer
   nor withhold his love from me.

■

AN INVITATION TO ALL THE EARTH!
   Celebrate!
   Give thanks!

FOR GOD'S HIGH DEEDS
   Come and see!
      —the passage of the Red Sea
      —the passage of the Jordan River

—our enemies have been vanquished
Bless our God!
    —he delivered us from our trials
    —he rescued from the burden of oppression

**BECAUSE OF THESE WONDROUS DEEDS, COME WITH
ME AND LET US OFFER A SACRIFICE OF THANKSGIVING!**
    Nothing is too good for our Lord!
    Come and listen!
    The Lord has done marvelous deeds for me.
    Blessed be God, the Lord of the Universe!

■

A FIRST READING: WITH ISRAEL

As in many other "Psalms of Thanksgiving," we have, first and foremost, a corporate prayer. Take notice of the "we" in the last seven stanzas. Israel remembers the marvelous deeds of the Exodus, especially the "passage through water," the "Passover" of the Red Sea and the Jordan River, both obstacles overcome by the grace of God. But this is also an individual prayer, and from stanza eight on, the psalmist switches to "I" because the "liberating deeds" God performed in the history of Israel are relevant to all distressing situations, even individual trials, in which God remains the same, the one who delivers.

From a poetic standpoint, let us notice the striking metaphors:

—the crucible in which metals are refined . . . in the same manner, suffering refines us.

—the snare, the heavy burden that crushes our backs . . . in the same manner, suffering is dreadful and can arrest all our efforts and kill our enthusiasm.

—the ordeals by water and fire . . . in the face of which we so often are helpless and through which we must nevertheless "pass."

A SECOND READING: WITH JESUS

Let us now reread this psalm with Jesus who "passed" from death to life by his resurrection. Jesus is the new Israel, the new Universal Being. Just as the Jews had to cross the Red Sea and the Jordan River, Jesus had to be tried in the crucible of the passion. No one more than he has offered a sacrifice of thanksgiving, no one more than he has invited the entire universe to share in his eucharist. On the redemptive role of suffering, Jesus had these words to say (in which he gave away the secret of his courageous soul): "Every branch in me that bears no fruit *he cuts away,* and every branch that does bear fruit *he prunes* to make it bear even *more!"* (Jn 15:2).

A THIRD READING: WITH OUR TIME

1. *"To Him I Cried Aloud . . . He Has Heeded the Voice of My Prayer."*—This is more than just an image, and at this very moment, "cries" are literally going up to the heavens from all the continents of our planet. The cry of those who hunger, the cry of those who are oppressed or persecuted, rejected or downtrodden, the cry of those who are helpless, the cry of the sick who are in pain, the moaning of those who are in the throes of death.

2. *"You, O God, Have Tested Us, You Have Tried Us As Silver Is Tried"*—O yes, I could ponder for a long time over this symbol of the "crucible of suffering." Sometimes, our contemporaries blame God for all the evils that make people cry. Let us listen to this accusation. Let us also listen to the beginning of an answer which is given to us in this psalm: maybe our trials are, after all, only a passage, a "passover" . . . like the fire that makes the melting gold groan in order to free it from its dross. We do know that trials are frightful and God himself tells us that we should not be afraid to pray for relief. But we also know that suffering has a mysterious power of purification which makes us grow, molds our character and renders us more sympathetic to the pain of others. Is this perhaps why God allows suffering, for the good that comes out of it?

3. *Praise! Celebrate! Sing! Come and See! Give Thanks!*—No, we are not delivered into the hands of the powers of hell! Evil is not a god! Only God is God! I believe in the victorious actions of God. I believe in resurrection and life eternal, and all the eucharists of my earthly life will not suffice to give thanks to God. Blessed be God who saves us!

PSALM 67

אֱלֹהִים יְחָנֵּנוּ

LET THE PEOPLES PRAISE YOU, O GOD!

2 O God, be gracious and bless us
   and let your face shed its light upon us.
3 So will your way be known upon earth
   and all nations learn your saving help.

4 Let the peoples praise you, O God;
   let all the peoples praise you.

5 Let the nations be glad and exult
   for you rule the world with justice.
   With fairness you rule the peoples,
   you guide the nations on earth.

6 Let the peoples praise you, O God;
   let all the peoples praise you.

7 The earth has yielded its fruit
   for God, our God, has blessed us.
8 May God still give us his blessing
   till the ends of the earth revere him.

   Let the peoples praise you, O God;
   let all the peoples praise you.

■

**Israel, as well as the whole earth,
is under the eye of God:**
   —the earth . . .
   —all the nations . . .

—all the peoples . . .
—everybody . . .

Let them rejoice . . .
Let them sing . . .
    —the peoples . . .
    —the nations of the earth . . .

Universal jubilation!
Universal eucharist!

Joy of the harvest:
May God bless us!
May He bless the entire earth!
Everywhere . . .

■

A FIRST READING: WITH ISRAEL

This is an especially jubilant "Psalm of Blessing." Once more, we see how much the people of Israel were aware of the extraordinary privilege they had received when they became the people of the Covenant and at the same time how eager they were to share this happiness with the whole of humankind. They wanted all men and women, all the nations, all the earth, to share in the blessings which they had been the first to enjoy. This psalm was probably sung during one of the harvest festivals: Pentecost or the Festival of the Tents. The fruitfulness of the earth and the success of a plentiful harvest prompted the Hebrews to share their happiness, the fruits of divine blessing.

A SECOND READING: WITH JESUS

"Go out to the whole world: proclaim the gospel to all creation . . ." (Mk 16:15–16). Jesus truly experienced the universality of Israel in his very soul. In fact, he was the One who transformed this desire into reality when he sent his disciples "till the ends of the earth." Jesus must have said this psalm with so much fervor!

"Thy universal kingdom come, thy will be done."—"Let the peoples praise you, O God, let all the peoples praise you!"

"The earth has yielded its fruit." Jesus, did not neglect this very realistic and very temporal dimension of happiness deeply rooted in earthly goods, and he did tell us to ask for "our daily bread."

"So will your way be known upon earth." Jesus claimed to be this way: "I am the Way, the Truth and the Life."

"Let your face shed its light upon us!" The radiant face of God . . . God's smile over the human race . . . Did not Jesus—through his incarnation—become the extraordinary answer to this prayer? The invisible God, the God "without a face" became visible to our eyes in the human face of Jesus!

"The earth has yielded its harvest, its fruit . . ." Jesus, the fruit of the earth! Jesus, the most wonderful harvest that ever sprang forth from the bosom of the earth!

"All nations will learn your saving power." This saving

power was brought by Jesus. When praying this psalm, Jesus was praying for his own mission, according to God's plan: "I did not come to bring condemnation, but salvation."

"You guide the nations on earth." To lead, to guide: a divine role. Jesus explicitly claimed this role when he presented himself as the "Good Shepherd" who leads his sheep toward springs of living water.

A THIRD READING: WITH OUR TIME

1. *The Entire Earth . . . The Whole World . . . All the Peoples . . . All Men and Women*—This cosmic, universal vision is very modern. Never before our time have people crossed so many borders and traveled to so many far-away lands. Thanks to television, the entire world comes to our house and the lives and problems of others become closer to us. At the same time dreams of lasting, universal peace are emphasized.

"Let the nations be glad and exult!" When we say this psalm, let us not lock ourselves in our own little world and our own narrow nationalism, but let us rather use this psalm to broaden our horizons.

2. *The Earth Has Yielded Its Fruit . . . God, Our God Gives Us His Blessing*—During certain periods of its history, the church has been tempted by a disincarnated spirituality and a contempt for worldly things which were considered impure. Let us not fall into the other extreme and idolize earthly goods. Jesus called the man who was building a bigger barn—to accommodate an exceptionally good harvest—a fool, not because of his success but because he neglected to think about his soul. Yes, earthly happiness is very fragile and can never satisfy our hunger and our thirst. But let us not forget that it is God who created the earth and its seasons, our bread and our wine. The true Christian attitude should be one of total dedication to the success of creation: harvesting a good crop, operating a business, completing a difficult task . . . all these are gifts from God. "God, our God has blessed us."

3. *Let the Nations Be Glad and Exult!*—We must seek joy and happiness. We must dare to pray in that direction, dare to ask God to increase our joy and our happiness. And if we truly

ask that all nations "be glad and exult," how can we possibly keep a glum face? Joy is the wonderful secret of Christian men and women, and "a sad saint" is indeed a "sorry saint!"

4. *A Prayer for the Harvest, A Prayer for the Autumn of Life* —Old age is not an easy time and fall is the season of nostalgia, but life goes on in the harvest that is being stored. Everything— work and love, sacrifice and self-denial in a human life is "stored in God," better than in any barn. What old people have accomplished in their lifetimes, the seeds that have been harvested will be used again at sowing time. For those who believe in God, nothing ever ends!

PSALM 68

THE GOD OF VICTORIES

2 Let God arise, let his foes be scattered.
Let those who hate him flee before him.
3 As smoke is blown away so will they be blown away;
like wax that melts before the fire,
so the wicked shall perish at the presence of God.

4 But the just shall rejoice at the presence of God,
they shall exult and dance for joy.
5 O sing to the Lord, make music to his name;
make a highway for him who rides on the clouds.
Rejoice in the Lord, exult at his presence.

6 Father of the orphan, defender of the widow,
such is God in his holy place.
7 God gives the lonely a home to live in;
he leads prisoners forth into freedom:
but rebels must dwell in a parched land.

8 When you went forth, O God, at the head of your people,
when you marched across the desert, the earth trembled:
the heavens melted at the presence of God,
at the presence of God, Israel's God.

10 You poured down, O God, a generous rain:
when your people were starved you gave them new life.
11 It was there that your people found a home,
prepared in your goodness, O God, for the poor.

12 The Lord gives the word to the bearers of good tidings:
"The Almighty has defeated a numberless army
13 and kings and armies are in flight, in flight
while you were at rest among the sheepfolds."

14 At home the women already share the spoil.
They are covered with silver as the wings of a dove,
its feathers brilliant with shining gold
15 and jewels flashing like snow on Mount Zalmon.

16 The mountains of Bashan are mighty mountains;
high-ridged mountains are the mountains of Bashan.
17 Why look with envy, you high-ridged mountains,
at the mountain where God has chosen to dwell?
It is there that the Lord shall dwell forever.

18 The chariots of God are thousands upon thousands.
The Lord has come from Sinai to the holy place.
19 You have gone up on high; you have taken captives,
receiving men in tribute, O God,
even those who rebel, into your dwelling, O Lord.

20 May the Lord be blessed day after day.
He bears our burdens, God our saviour.
21 This God of ours is a God who saves.
The Lord our God holds the keys of death.
22 And God will smite the head of his foes,
the crown of those who persist in their sins.

23 The Lord said: "I will bring them back from Bashan;
I will bring them back from the depth of the sea.
24 Then your feet will tread in their blood
and the tongues of your dogs take their share of the foe."

25 They see your solemn procession, O God,
the procession of my God, of my king, to the sanctuary:
26 the singers in the forefront, the musicians coming last,
between them, maidens sounding their timbrels.

27 "In festive gatherings, bless the Lord;
bless God, O you who are Israel's sons."
28 There is Benjamin, least of the tribes, at the head,
Judah's princes, a mighty throng,
Zebulun's princes, Naphtali's princes.

29   Show forth, O God, show forth your might,
      your might, O God, which you have shown for us
30   for the sake of your temple high in Jerusalem
      may kings come to you bringing their tribute.

31   Threaten the wild beast that dwells in the reeds,
      the bands of the mighty and lords of the peoples.
      Let them bow down offering silver.
      Scatter the peoples who delight in war.
32   Princes will make their way from Egypt:
      Ethiopia will stretch out her hands to God.

33   Kingdoms of the earth, sing to God, praise the Lord
34   who rides on the heavens, the ancient heavens.
      He thunders his voice, his mighty voice.
35   Come, acknowledge the power of God.

      His glory is on Israel; his might is in the skies.
36   God is to be feared in his holy place.
      He is the Lord, Israel's God.
      He gives strength and power to his people.

      Blessed be God!

■

An epic,
A grandiose theophany.

Throughout history . . .
God is leading his people in a victorious march
toward the final, eschatological triumph.

> **God of Love,**
> **Father of the orphan,**
> **Defender of the widow,**
> **Liberator of the oppressed.**

Leaving Egypt, the land of slavery . . .
    Mount Sinai . . .
    the manna . . .
    the long march . . .

God is merciful to the poor
    the conquest of Canaan

God does not choose the mighty, but the humble
    he chose Mount Zion to erect his temple
    his victories dot history

The victory parade,
the joyous procession . . .

The universal ascent of all humankind toward Jerusalem . . .

Universal peace . . .

Universal adoration . . .

All of history is summed up in the interventions of God on behalf of his people, for the poor and the humble.

The word *Elohim* (= God) is used thirty-two times;
the word *Yahweh* (= the Lord) is used ten times.

■

A FIRST READING: WITH ISRAEL

This "Psalm of the Kingdom" is an epic ode which celebrates "God-King." The background is that of a fantastic celebration of victory. After a victorious battle, the king returns to his capital and goes up to the temple to give thanks, escorted by his people giving shouts of joy.

We find here many allusions to the history of Israel.

A SECOND READING: WITH JESUS

We must go beyond the grandiose images of this epic poem and read it with our hearts, as an interpretation of history. The "God of the poor, Father of the orphan, defender of the widow" puts all his powers of "Horseman of the Clouds" at the service of the ones he loves—and he crushes their enemies to dust. The great victory of this God is the *cross* of Jesus! The triumph of the King, his victory procession is his ascent into heaven on *Ascension* Day! The true ascent of the nations to Jerusalem is the *Pentecost* of the church. The land promised to all men and women is nothing less than this sanctuary where God himself dwells: his own *eternal life*. All of this certainly deserves the exalted style of this triumphant march!

A THIRD READING: WITH OUR TIME

More than any other period, our modern time is very sensitive to the meaning of history. This psalm tells us where humankind is headed: political convulsions, shifting of powers, wars, bloody violence, oppression of all kinds, sin, and death. . . . All of this leads to the "fulfilment of history" which shall see the victory of *love,* for "the Lord, our God, holds the keys of death." History does not make sense without the central "event" which is at its very heart: the resurrection of Jesus Christ.

Vexilla regis prodeunt, fulget crucis mysterium—"The king's standards move forward and the mystery of the cross is resplendent."

Blessed be God! Arise, O Lord, and save us!

PSALM 69

FROM THE WATERS OF THE DEEP

2   Save me, O God,
for the waters have risen to my neck.

3   I have sunk into the mud of the deep
and there is no foothold.
I have entered the waters of the deep
and the waves overwhelm me.

4   I am wearied with all my crying.
my throat is parched.
My eyes are wasted away
from looking for my God.

5   More numerous than the hairs on my head
are those who hate me without cause.
Those who attack me with lies
are too much for my strength.

How can I restore
what I have never stolen?
6   O God, you know my sinful folly;
my sins you can see.

7   Let those who hope in you not be put to shame
through me, Lord of hosts:
let not those who seek you be dismayed
through me, God of Israel.

8   It is for you that I suffer taunts,
that shame covers my face,
9   that I have become a stranger to my brothers,
an alien to my own mother's sons.

10   I burn with zeal for your house
    and taunts against you fall on me.

11   When I afflict my soul with fasting
    they make it a taunt against me.
12   When I put on sackcloth in mourning
    then they make me a byword,
13   the gossip of men at the gates,
    the subject of drunkards' songs.

14   This is my prayer to you,
    my prayer for your favour.
    In your great love, answer me, O God,
    with your help that never fails:
15   rescue me from sinking in the mud;
    save me from my foes.

    Save me from the waters of the deep
16   lest the waves overwhelm me.
    Do not let the deep engulf me
    nor death close its mouth on me.

17   Lord, answer, for your love is kind;
    in your compassion, turn towards me.
18   Do not hide your face from your servant;
    answer quickly for I am in distress.
19   Come close to my soul and redeem me;
    ransom me pressed by my foes.

20   You know how they taunt and deride me;
    my oppressors are all before you.
21   Taunts have broken my heart;
    I have reached the end of my strength.
    I looked in vain for compassion,
    for consolers; not one could I find.

22   For food they gave me poison;
    in my thirst they gave me vinegar to drink.
23   Let their table be a snare to them
    and their festive banquets a trap.

24 Let their eyes grow dim and blind;
   let their limbs tremble and shake.

25 Pour out your anger upon them,
   let the heat of your fury overtake them.
26 Let their camp be left desolate;
   let no one dwell in their tents:
27 for they prosecute one whom you struck;
   they increase the pain of him you wounded.

28 Charge them with guilt upon guilt;
   let them never be found just in your sight.
29 Blot them out from the book of the living;
   do not enrol them among the just.
30 As for me in poverty and pain
   let your help, O God, lift me up.

31 I will praise God's name with a song;
   I will glorify him with thanksgiving.
32 A gift pleasing God more than oxen,
   more than beasts prepared for sacrifice.

33 The poor when they see it will be glad
   and God-seeking hearts will revive;
34 for the Lord listens to the needy
   and does not spurn his servants in their chains.
35 Let the heavens and the earth give him praise,
   the sea and all its living creatures.

36 For God will bring help to Zion
   and rebuild the cities of Judah
   and men shall dwell there in possession.
37 The sons of his servants shall inherit it;
   those who love his name shall dwell there.

■

A FIRST READING: WITH ISRAEL

This messianic psalm is composed of three laments:

1. *The Supplicant Utters A Cry of Distress:*

—Horrible suffering: he is asphyxiated by waves of mud, he is screaming and his throat is on fire.

—Unjust suffering: he is being persecuted because of his piety, he is being swallowed by the ambient paganism.

—Suffering for the cause of God—"I burn with zeal for your house and taunts against you fall on me."

—Numerous enemies surround him.

2. *Instead of Giving Up, The Supplicant Turns towards God and Prays:*

—He begs for deliverance and salvation.

—He demands revenge according to the law of retaliation, and it is toward the powers of hell that his terrible imprecations are directed. He asks God to eradicate them: May all of God's enemies be destroyed!

3. *This Dramatic Supplication Ends in A Prayer of Thanksgiving:* The cries and the imprecations of the first two parts must be understood in the light of the finale: "I will praise God's name . . . the poor will be glad . . . God-seeking hearts will revive . . . the Lord listens to the needy."

A SECOND READING: WITH JESUS

Psalm 69 is one of the psalms most quoted in the New Testament.

—In the anger of Jesus against the merchants of the temple the disciples recognized the application of this verse: "I burn with zeal for your house" (Jn 2:17).

—Jesus explicitly quoted this psalm the day before his passion when he talked about his enemies: "they hate me without cause" (Jn 15:25).

—"In my thirst they gave me vinegar to drink" (Jn 19:28). The evangelist tells us that Jesus said: "I am thirsty," in order that the scripture would be fulfilled.

—Even the imprecations were quoted by the early Christians and applied to Judas' treason (Ac 1:20; Rm 11:9, Rm 15:3), thus alluding to the mystery of the iniquity of the world.

This righteous man who suffers for God's cause, like Job or Jeremiah, is first an "anonymous poor" from the Old Testament, but he is also—in an eminent way—Jesus on the cross. And it is not by chance that the finale becomes a song of thanksgiving. When Jesus rehearsed his death—the night before—he was experiencing it freely, like a eucharistic meal.

A THIRD READING: WITH OUR TIME

1. *There Is A Burning Actuality in These Laments:* "Save me, O God . . . I am sinking . . . I am exhausted . . . my eyes are worn out . . . my enemies are numerous . . . I am crying . . . Insults fall upon me." This is the prayer of those who are sick and afflicted, but it is also the collective prayer of the Third World countries. If we try to reread this psalm while putting it in the mouths of these people, maybe we will understand why the temptation of revolutionary violence inhabits their hearts; and maybe we will become more involved in improving the quality of their lives through prayer and action.

2. *"God Will Bring Help to Zion and Rebuild the Cities of Judah . . . for the Lord Listens to the Needy"*—"Jesus" in Hebrew means "God saves." This psalm can help us to better pray for the salvation of the world. . . .

3. *To Hope, to Wait*—Hope is one of the values our contemporary society needs the most. For a while the progress of technology seemed to have taken the place of hope. For a while, men and women were intoxicated by their scientific victories and they may have thought that the old religious idea of hope had become obsolete . . . Why should we turn to God when we can obtain "everything" through our own strength? But the scientific age has not solved many of the calamities which burden the human condition: emotional fragility, new gaps in relationships between generations and social classes, anxiety and loneliness, fear of the future, etc. . . . All of these have created a renewed need for hope. Each one of us must adapt the formulas of this psalm to his or her particular living conditions: "Save me, O God . . . let those who hope in you not be put to shame . . . Come close to my soul and redeem me!"

4. *For A "Moving" Prayer*—If we follow the "movement" of

the psalm we are struck by its truth-filled dynamism. It starts with a cry, continues with a plea, and ends in joyful thanksgiving. This is the movement we must follow when we pray. Our prayer should not be a fussy, static rehashing of our problems and pains. A true prayer should transform us and help us "move" forward. It is normal to start by exposing our troubles to God like the touching lament at the beginning of this psalm, but we should also attain its finale: "I will praise God's name with a song . . . Let the heavens and the earth give him praise . . . God-seeking hearts will revive . . . The poor will be glad!"

PSALM 71

בְּךָ־יְהוָה חָסִיתִי

YOU WILL GIVE ME BACK MY LIFE

1 In you, O Lord, I take refuge;
 let me never be put to shame.
2 In your justice rescue me, free me:
 pay heed to me and save me.

3 Be a rock where I can take refuge,
 a mighty stronghold to save me;
 for you are my rock, my stronghold.
4 Free me from the hand of the wicked,
 from the grip of the unjust, of the oppressor.

5 It is you, O Lord, who are my hope,
 my trust, O Lord, since my youth.
6 On you I have leaned from my birth,
 from my mother's womb you have been my help.
 My hope has always been in you.

7 My fate has filled many with awe
 but you are my strong refuge.
8 My lips are filled with your praise,
 with your glory all the day long.
9 Do not reject me now that I am old;
 when my strength fails do not forsake me.

10 For my enemies are speaking about me;
 those who watch me take counsel together
11 saying: 'God has forsaken him; follow him,
 seize him; there is no one to save him.'
12 O God, do not stay far off:
 my God, make haste to help me!

13 Let them be put to shame and destroyed,
    all those who seek my life.
    Let them be covered with shame and confusion,
    all those who seek to harm me.

14 But as for me, I will always hope
    and praise you more and more.
15 My lips will tell of your justice
    and day by day of your help
    (though I can never tell it all).

16 I will declare the Lord's mighty deeds
    proclaiming your justice, yours alone.
17 O God, you have taught me from my youth
    and I proclaim your wonders still.

18 Now that I am old and grey-headed,
    do not forsake me, God.
    Let me tell of your powers to all ages,
    praise your strength and justice to the skies,
    tell of you who have worked such wonders.
    O God, who is like you?

20 You have burdened me with bitter troubles
    but you will give me back my life.
    You will raise me from the depths of the earth;
21 You will exalt me and console me again.

22 So I will give you thanks on the lyre
    for your faithful love, my God.
    To you I will sing with the harp
    to you, the Holy One of Israel.
23 When I sing to you my lips shall rejoice
    and my soul, which you have redeemed.

24 And all the day long my tongue
    shall tell the tale of your justice:
    for they are put to shame and disgraced,
    all those who seek to harm me.

■

SUPPLICATION . . .
>   —rescue me
>   —save me
>   —listen to me
>   —save me
>   —protect me
>   —rescue me

You are—my rock
>   —my stronghold
>   —my hope
>   —my God
>   —my help
>   —my protection

You loved me first,
>   —my refuge
>   —my strength

I want to praise *You!*

OF AN OLD MAN . . .
—whose strength is declining,
—who is surrounded by murderous enemies
—but who cries out to God,
—wishing for the destruction of these evil forces,
—who does not cease to *hope* and *pray.*

WHO EXPECTS A NEW LIFE FROM GOD
—for the present
—and for the future

You will let me *live* again,
you will *console* me again,

Then, with the harp and the lyre,
I will give you thanks . . .

My lips shall rejoice . . .

Praise and Joy forever!

■

A FIRST READING: WITH ISRAEL

As we have often noticed, the pronoun "I" which is used here actually represents Israel. This prayer, which is apparently very personal (and even individualistic) in its intimate tone is, in reality, a kind a parable. The people of Israel is presented as an old man, chosen by God even before he was born, and who tried to be faithful until his hair turned gray, a weak old man whose foes want to harm him. This man does not only ask God to prolong his poor, diminished life, but to give him a new life, a restored youth, a true resurrection. Then he will joyfully sing and praise the Lord.

From a literary standpoint, let us notice the movement of the psalm which—like a spiral—constantly mingles supplication and praise. The worshipper cries and moans but yet he never despairs, and while he begs the Lord he also gives thanks to him.

A SECOND READING: WITH JESUS

From the time he was a child, Jesus was always taking care of his Father's business. More than any other human being he could truly say: "From my mother's womb you have been my help . . . My fate has filled many with awe . . . My lips were filled with your praise, with your glory all the day long."

During his passion, Jesus asked to be delivered from his enemies: "My God, my God, why have you forsaken me? . . . The man is calling on Elijah . . . Wait and see if Elijah will come to save him!" (Mt 27:47–50).

But yet, even in this desperate situation, he always had the assurance of vindication: "You will give me back my life. You will save me from the depths of the earth. . . . When I sing to you my lips shall rejoice and my soul, which you have redeemed."

Yes, we must sing this psalm with Jesus!

A THIRD READING: WITH OUR TIME

1. *The Theme of Old Age*—The more we know how to cure diseases, the more helpless we feel at not being able to cure

death. The more well-being science brings us, the more difficult it becomes to leave this life. We must perhaps experience this terrible feeling of abandonment, of being rejected like an old tool that is no longer in working condition. We must perhaps come to terms with the cruel fact that a "certain kind of life" has ended and that old times will never come back . . . in order to truly share in the *hope* of the psalmist. The physical and biological rules of aging have no hold on the true believer who is waiting to receive *divine life*. Our new youth is still ahead of us—in God—This is where Joy is.

2. *The Will to Live*—God has infused us with a desire to live. This entire psalm protests against devitalization and physical diminishment in the name of God's eternal love. Since God created us out of love, how could he possibly forsake us? The resurrection of the dead is part of the original plan of the Creator. Let us not blame God for having created a "mortal" being, his plan is for a "resurrected" being!

3. *Praising*—Even in the midst of the most trying situations the psalmist keeps praising.

Let us follow his example, let us "take our lyre" and give thanks to God!

PSALM 72 אֱלֹהִים מִשְׁפָּטֶיךָ לְמֶלֶךְ תֵּן

BEFORE HIM ALL KINGS SHALL FALL PROSTRATE

1 O God, give your judgement to the king,
   to a king's son your judgement,
2 that he may judge your people with justice
   and your poor in right judgement.

3 May the mountains bring forth peace for the people
   and the hills, justice.
4 May he defend the poor of the people
   and save the children of the needy
   (and crush the oppressor).

5 He shall endure like the sun and the moon
   from age to age.
6 He shall descend like rain on the meadow,
   like raindrops on the earth.

7 In his days justice shall flourish
   and peace till the moon fails.
8 He shall rule from sea to sea,
   from the Great River to the earth's bounds.

9 Before him his enemies shall fall,
   his foes lick the dust.
10 The kings of Tarshish and the sea coasts
   shall pay him tribute.

   The kings of Sheba and Seba
   shall bring him gifts.
11 Before him all kings shall fall prostrate,
   all nations shall serve him.

12 For he shall save the poor when they cry
    and the needy who are helpless.
13 He will have pity on the weak
    and save the lives of the poor.

14 From oppression he will rescue their lives,
    to him their blood is dear.
15 (Long may he live,
    may the gold of Sheba be given him.)
    They shall pray for him without ceasing
    and bless him all the day.

16 May corn be abundant in the land
    to the peaks of the mountains.
    May its fruits rustle like Lebanon;
    may men flourish in the cities
    like grass on the earth.

17 May his name be blessed for ever
    and endure like the sun.
    Every tribe shall be blessed in him,
    all nations bless his name.

* * *

18 Blessed be the Lord, God of Israel,
    who alone works wonders,
19 ever blessed his glorious name.
    Let his glory fill the earth.

Amen! Amen!

■

A Prayer to the Messianic King:
  1. KING OF JUSTICE
  2. DEFENDER OF THE POOR

3. KING OF PEACE
1. and KING OF JUSTICE
2. and DEFENDER OF THE POOR
4. VICTOR OVER EVIL
5. ETERNAL KING
6. BENEFICENT KING
1. and KING OF JUSTICE
3. and KING OF PEACE AND PROSPERITY
7. UNIVERSAL KING
4. VICTOR OVER EVIL
7. and UNIVERSAL KING
2. and KING OF THE POOR
4. SAVING KING
2. DEFENDER OF THE POOR
5. ETERNAL KING
6. WHO BRINGS WITH HIM HAPPINESS AND PROSPERITY
5. MAY HE REIGN FOREVER!
6. MAY ALL RECOGNIZE HIM!

Blessed Be God Who Promises All These Wonders!

■

A FIRST READING: WITH ISRAEL

This psalm, written after the Exile, when David's dynasty no longer existed, alludes directly to the Messiah-King, to the messianic kingdom which will be "universal and eternal." Only God's reign can "last as long as the sun, for ever and ever." It would be presumptuous for any human king to aspire to this! As in the other psalms, we find here the literary device called *hofstil:* a metaphorical language which uses the style of the royal courts of the Orient, with its glorious hyperboles and its royal ideology, to tell us about a mystery, "to clothe" a revelation, not about a political system, but about God himself.

A SECOND READING: WITH JESUS

No psalm could be more fitting than this one to celebrate the Feast of Epiphany. It is like a prophecy announcing the Magi: "The Kings of Sheba and Seba shall bring him gifts." But beyond the concrete details of the genre, it is the entire psalm that alludes to Jesus, the friend and protector of the poor, the defender of the needy, the conqueror of the evil which makes our enemies—sin and death—"lick the dust." There is no other king besides him! Only one kingdom is eternal: his kingdom, the kingdom of love without frontiers, and we are invited to take part in its "advent."—*Adveniat regnum tuum . . .* Thy kingdom come!"

    We can imagine Jesus singing this psalm with his compatriots in the synagogue of his small village. The unknown carpenter was in all likelihood praying that God's rule would extend "from sea to sea," and that "every tribe (would) be blessed in him."

A THIRD READING: WITH OUR TIME

1. *From Sea to Sea . . . All the Nations . . . All the Races . . .*—Is my heart big enough? Or do I remain confined in my small stagnant universe? God's plan is universal. Thanks to television, the whole universe is at our door and I *can* make a difference in India or in Africa through my prayers and my commitment.

2. *"Before Him His Enemies Shall Fall, His Foes Lick the Dust."*—Evil must disappear. Exploitation of Man by Man must cease. . . .

Why is it that those who are putting into practice the message of the psalms and of the gospel are accused of being Marxists? How can Christians remain uninvolved in the fight against evil?

3. *"Justice . . . Justice . . . Justice . . ."*—The yearning for social justice that fills this psalm has always existed and always will. But it is especially urgent in our time. So much the better! But what do we do to make it happen? There are one thousand and one places where justice should reign: our family, our workplace, international relations. . . . Do we fulfil our workload honestly? Do we pay fair wages? Are we just with our family and friends, our co-workers?

4. *"The Poor . . . the Needy . . . the Weak . . ."*—Justice does not mean keeping the scale balanced, but tipping it in favor of all those who are the most exposed to the cruel blows of injustice. The King-Jesus-Messiah took the side of the poor. . . . What about us?

5. *"Abundance . . . the Gold of Sheba . . . Wheat Growing to the Peaks of the Mountains . . ."*—These are metaphors of fecundity and happiness, material images which are symbols of a spiritual happiness, of the messianic happiness: *peace.* Give us peace, O Lord, give peace—*shalom*—to all the earth!

6. *We Are All Responsible*—Nowadays, there are not many kings in the strict sense of the word, and this "prayer for the king" may seem outdated to many of us. Should we therefore store it in some museum of antiquities? Why could we not instead pray it "with our time?"

We do have fewer kings but we have more and more leaders at many different levels. Let us pray for them, that they may govern with justice, judge the poor with right judgment, defend the poor, save the children of the needy, that they may fight oppression and violence and promote peace and prosperity!

7. *The King Is Not the King*—Israel gives us a valuable lesson for all times and all political systems: in the Bible, the king is

not the king! *God* is the King! Under the guise of a regime similar to that of its neighbors, Israel was, in fact, living under a truly original political system, neither monarchy nor democracy, but a theocracy.

There is somebody "above" all those in power, and they cannot therefore govern as they please, nor for their own benefit.

Only God is king!

PSALM 80 רֹעֵה יִשְׂרָאֵל הַאֲזִינָה

GOD OF HOSTS, BRING US BACK

2   O shepherd of Israel, hear us,
    you who lead Joseph's flock,
    shine forth from your cherubim throne
3   upon Ephraim, Benjamin, Manasseh.
    O Lord, rouse up your might,
    O Lord, come to our help.

4   God of hosts, bring us back;
       let your face shine on us and we shall be saved.

5   Lord God of hosts, how long
    will you frown on your people's plea?
6   You have fed them with tears for their bread,
    an abundance of tears for their drink.
7   You have made us the taunt of our neighbours,
    our enemies laugh us to scorn.

8   God of hosts, bring us back;
       let your face shine on us and we shall be saved.

9   You brought a vine out of Egypt;
    to plant it you drove out the nations.
10 Before it you cleared the ground;
    it took root and spread through the land.

11 The mountains were covered with its shadow,
    the cedars of God with its boughs.
12 It stretched out its branches to the sea,
    to the Great River it stretched out its shoots.

13 Then why have you broken down its walls?
   It is plucked by all who pass by.
14 It is ravaged by the boar of the forest,
   devoured by the beasts of the field.

15 God of hosts, turn again, we implore,
   look down from heaven and see.
   Visit this vine and protect it,
   the vine your right hand has planted.
17 Men have burnt it with fire and destroyed it.
   May they perish at the frown of your face.

18 May your hand be on the man you have chosen,
   the man you have given your strength.
19 And we shall never forsake you again:
   give us life that we may call upon your name.

20 God of hosts, bring us back;
   let your face shine on us and we shall be saved.

■

GOD'S FLOCK
   calls its shepherd!
   —listen to us
   —shine forth
   —rouse up your might
   —come
   —bring us back
   Why **do you no longer listen to our prayers?**
   Why **this abundance of tears?**
   Why **are our enemies triumphing over us?**

GOD'S VINE
   once the object of His loving care . . .
   now . . . abandoned

—**turn again**
—**look down from heaven**
—**protect us**
—**give us life**

And We Shall Be Saved!

■

A FIRST READING: WITH ISRAEL

"O Shepherd of Israel, come and save your flock!" How beautiful is this image of the shepherd who watches over his sheep and leads them to green pastures! The King of Israel par excellence was David, the poor shepherd from Bethlehem.

In this psalm, it is God who is called "the shepherd" as so many prophets have foretold (Jr 31:10; Is 40:11; Ezk: 34).

"The *Vine* your right hand has planted . . ." This is another traditional and beautiful metaphor: the vine is a plant which requires much care. The love of the vine-tender for the vine is one of the images of the love of God for his people (Is 5:1–7; Jr 2:21, 5:10, 12:10; Ezk 15:1–8; Ho 10:1).

A SECOND READING: WITH JESUS

"I am the good shepherd . . . I know my sheep" (Jn 10:1–21).

"I am the vine . . . you are the branches" (Jn 15:1–8).

Let us look at the refrain of this psalm: "God of hosts, bring us back; let your face shine on us and we shall be saved." Jesus himself is God's answer to this prayer. The very name "Jesus" means "God saves." And Jesus is truly the "face" of God, the only face we can see." No one has ever seen God; it is the only Son, who is close to the Father's heart, who has made him known" (Jn 1:18).

"Let your face shine . . . let your face smile!" Jesus is the face of God, smiling at the sinner, he is the face that saves: "I came to call not the upright, but the sinners" (Jn 9:12).

A THIRD READING: WITH OUR TIME

1. *A Corporate Supplication*—*We* are oppressed, Lord! Save *us!* We must say this psalm in the plural, in the name of all those men and women who have shed too many tears for their bread: "You have fed them with tears for their bread, an abundance of tears for their drink."

2. *"Lord, How Long Will You Frown On Your People's Plea?"*—This is an amazingly bold question. God does not "frown" on our *questions,* instead he "suggests" them to us.

Asking questions of God is also a form of prayer. "Why, God? . . . Why is there so much suffering in the world? . . ."—"Rouse up your might . . . come to our help!"

A world without God is a world without hope. The incarnation which we celebrate at Christmas is *the Advent of God, the Advent of love in our world.* Christmas is not only the celebration of a baby's birthday, it is the actualization in today's world of the birth of a God who wants "to be born" unceasingly.

3. *A World in Crisis—A Church in Crisis*—"Why have you broken down its walls? It is plucked by all who pass by. It is ravaged by the boar of the forest, devoured by the beasts of the field." At that time in Israel, there was a schism between the tribes of the north and the tribes of the south. Today, we still have the same conflict between the north and the south, the rich and the poor . . . We still have conflicts between social classes, between religions, and between races. Nothing is protected any more: walls are broken down, everything is being plucked and ravaged.

Faced with this depressing reality, the psalmist *is Sorrowful but not despairing* . . . He turns to God and prays: "Come back, O Lord, show us your face, smile upon us!" He knows that his prayer will be answered and he promises to give thanks to God: "We shall never forsake *you* again: give us life that we may call upon *your* name!"

PSALM 90

אֲדֹנָי מָעוֹן אַחָה

MAKE US KNOW THE SHORTNESS OF OUR LIFE

1   O Lord, you have been our refuge
    from one generation to the next.
2   Before the mountains were born
    or the earth or the world brought forth,
    you are God, without beginning or end.

3   You turn men back into dust
    and say: "Go back, sons of men."
4   To your eyes a thousand years
    are like yesterday, come and gone,
    no more than a watch in the night.

5   You sweep men away like a dream,
    like grass which springs up in the morning.
6   In the morning it springs up and flowers:
    by evening it withers and fades.

7   So we are destroyed in your anger
    struck with terror in your fury.
8   Our guilt lies open before you;
    our secrets in the light of your face.

9   All our days pass away in your anger.
    Our life is over like a sigh.
10 Our span is seventy years
    or eighty for those who are strong.

    And most of these are emptiness and pain.
    They pass swiftly and we are gone.
11 Who understands the power of your anger
    and fears the strength of your fury?

12   Make us know the shortness of our life
     that we might gain wisdom of heart.
13   Lord, relent! Is your anger for ever?
     Show pity to your servants.

14   In the morning, fill us with your love;
     we shall exult and rejoice all our days.
15   Give us joy to balance our affliction
     for the years when we knew misfortune.

16   Show forth your work to your servants;
     let your glory shine on their children.
17   Let the favour of the Lord be upon us:
     give success to the work of our hands
     (give success to the work of our hands).

■

GOD IS ETERNAL...
  right away, an affirmation of faith:
 —You are our refuge.

 —image of the stability of the mountains: before them, *you are!*

MEN AND WOMEN ARE EPHEMERAL...
 —insignificant specks of dust...
 —like dreams...
 —like grass...
 —like fragile flowers...

OUR SINS
 —increase our misery,
 —add to the tragedy of the human condition

BUT THERE IS HOPE
 since we have *prayer*...
 —teach us your wisdom...

—relent . . .
—love . . . joy . . . singing . . .
—show forth the work of your hands . . .
—give success to the work of our hands . . .

■

A FIRST READING: WITH ISRAEL

The superscription of this psalm attributes it to: "Moses, Man of God." It is the only psalm attributed to Moses—perhaps because of its literary contacts with (1) Genesis: "For dust you are and to dust you shall return" (Gn 3:19), (2) with Exodus: "Give up your burning wrath" (Ex 32:12) and (3) with the Canticle of Moses in Deuteronomy 32.

It is a collective prayer of supplication and the psalmist uses plural pronouns: he prays not only for his own sins but for the sins of the entire nation, with an admirable sense of community!

This psalm was used by the Hebrews as a penitential prayer, to ask for the forgiveness of sins.

Note the poetic, concrete images: the striking comparison between the permanence and stable strength of the mountains and the ephemeral beauty of the flowers, blooming at dawn and wilted by dusk; or the nocturnal dream which we can no longer remember when we awake. In "The Dream of Gerontius," Newman puts this psalm on the lips of those who are suffering in purgatory. Before him, Bossuet had already used these same images in his meditations on youth and death. The heartrending melancholy expressed here is one of the themes used in all literatures.

A SECOND READING: WITH JESUS

Jesus asked a young man to leave everything and follow him. Had he done so, he would have freed himself from his ephemeral wealth and entered into eternity—on this earth. Jesus told us how foolish it is to stake everything on earthly values: "This very night the demand will be made for your soul; and this hoard of yours, whose will it be then?" (Lk 12:20). Just like the psalmist, our Lord also invited us to build our lives not on sand but on rock (Mt 7:26).

For the Hebrews, any affliction was perceived as chastisement from God for their sins, and the "anger" of God is at the center of this psalm. Jesus added important nuances to this issue. Saying that all suffering is punishment from God is erroneous; this is the significance of the Book of Job. It is also what Jesus said in his response concerning the man who was born blind: "Neither he nor his parents sinned" (Jn 9:3). Suffering, nevertheless, serves as a reminder of human frailty, and when asked about the people "on whom the tower at Siloam fell, killing them all," Jesus said that "they were not guiltier than those who were not killed"; but he did add: "unless you repent you will all perish" (Lk 13:4–5).

A THIRD READING: WITH OUR TIME

1. *Is Our Life Meaningless?*—The ideas expressed in this psalm are akin to those of many modern philosophers who stress the "absurdity" of the human condition. The psalmist already said that *"Man is not"* but *"God is."* And he was bold enough to call upon this strong God and to rely on *him.* The sign of our greatness as human beings is precisely that we are bold enough to think that we can "give" something to God:

—by our *wisdom,* which he imparted to us and which lies in understanding the brevity of our days on earth so that we may live them to the fullest,

—by our *praise* which allows us to sing for God,

—by our *work* which God makes fruitful.

2. *Our Sins*—Why could we not use our sins as a basis for prayer, with the help of this psalm? They are, after all, the manifestation of our deepest weaknesses. How could we resent the fact that the Holy God unrelentingly pursues evil to the innermost recesses of our consciences where "our shameful secrets lie exposed before God's face?" Since the death of Christ we know the price God has paid as he fights the battle against evil for us. God's anger is not directed *against* the sinner but *against* Satan and *for* the sinner: "Indeed I came to call not the upright, but sinners" (Mt 9:13).

3. *Human Freedom and Divine Grace*—What a beautiful, well-balanced formula! Let us ponder it! . . . "Give success (here is the role of divine grace) to the work of our hands (there is the role of human freedom). We cannot possibly extricate ourselves from sin on our own (see the entire Letter to the Romans). We need the conjunction of two forces: God and me; *His* grace and *my* efforts.

PSALM 91  יֵשֵׁב בְּסֵתֶר עֶלְיוֹן

IN THE SHELTER OF THE MOST HIGH

1 He who dwells in the shelter of the Most High
and abides in the shade of the Almighty
2 says to the Lord: "My refuge,
my stronghold, my God in whom I trust!"

3 It is he who will free you from the snare
of the fowler who seeks to destroy you;
4 he will conceal you with his pinions
and under his wings you will find refuge.

5 You will not fear the terror of the night
nor the arrow that flies by day,
6 nor the plague that prowls in the darkness
nor the scourge that lays waste at noon.

7 A thousand may fall at your side,
ten thousand fall at your right,
you, it will never approach;
his faithfulness is buckler and shield.

8 Your eyes have only to look
to see how the wicked are repaid,
9 you who have said: "Lord, my refuge!"
and have made the most high your dwelling.

10 Upon you no evil shall fall,
no plague approach where you dwell.
11 For you he has commanded his angels,
to keep you in all your ways.

12 They shall bear you upon their hands
lest you strike your foot against a stone.

13   On the lion and the viper you will tread
     and trample the young lion and the dragon.

14   "Since he clings to me in love, I will free him;
     protect him for he knows my name.
15   When he calls I shall answer: 'I am with you.'
     I will save him in distress and give him glory.

16   With length of life I will content him;
     I shall let him see my saving power."

∎

EXCLAMATION OF THE PILGRIM who seeks shelter and comes to spend the night in the temple.

RESPONSE OF THE PRIESTS who describe the protection that will surround the supplicant.

THE ORACLE OF GOD speaks:
    I will protect him . . .
    I will save him . . .
    I will remain by his side . . .
    I will rescue him . . .
    I will give him eternal life . . .
    I will let him "see" my salvation

∎

A FIRST READING: WITH ISRAEL

In Hebrew, the verb "to abide" used in the second verse means "to spend the night in the shade of the Almighty." The king of Israel comes to spend a night of prayer in the temple, just like Solomon who spent the night at Gibeon (1K 3:4–15), or like Saul who solicited an oracle before fighting a decisive battle (1S 28:5–6). The change of personal pronouns in the text gives us an indication of who the different protagonists are. First, the king arrives in front of the temple and explains his intent. Then, the priests of the holy place welcome him and tell him how he must trust in God's protection. Toward the end of this night of prayer, God speaks in a solemn oracle and tells the king that he will be victorious. It is now time for the king to return to the battle-field . . .

A SECOND READING: WITH JESUS

After forty days of fasting and prayer spent in the desert in communion with the Father, Jesus was tempted by *evil*. Satan quoted this psalm to him: "Throw yourself down; for scripture says: 'He has given his angels orders about you, and they will carry you in their arms in case you trip over a stone' " (Mt 4:5–6). Jesus truly "prayed" this psalm; actually he "lived" it.

The final oracle in this psalm makes sense only when it is applied to Jesus. The matter in question here is the great battle of Jesus against sin and death—against the Dragon, the Snake, the Devil, Satan (Rv 20:2)—Even though the forces of evil may break loose, the promised victory is at hand: "You shall trample the dragon! I want to save and protect you, I am with you. I will deliver and glorify you. I want to bless you with a long life. I will reveal my *salvation* to you." This psalm sings of the resurrection: it is Christ's victory song.

A THIRD READING: WITH OUR TIME

1. *Evil Surrounds Us*—but God is present at the heart of history, and one day evil will be eradicated for ever and we will be partners in God's victory. The abundance of the successive

images gives us an idea of the extent of the struggle: "the fowler's snare, the terror of the night, the arrow that flies by night, the plague that prowls in the darkness, the scourge that lays waste at noon, the lion, the viper, the *dragon.*" This last word truly names the evil. We know that it is not a minor skirmish, but a battle between God and the Adversary. Our modern world knows that evil is multiform, omnipotent, cunning or violent, and everyone of us can put concrete situations under the words of this psalm.

2. *Lent* could also be an opportunity for us to spend such a "night" of recollection, a night "in the shade of the Almighty," a night of vigil before the fight, similar to the night Jesus experienced before entering the lists for his great battle.

Let us not forget that we are not fighting against just any adversary but against *The Adversary,* the Dragon of the Apocalypse. Yes, fight we must, but before the battle we need to revive our strength in the presence of our God.

3. *God's Victory—What Is It?*—It is the decisive eschatological victory which is already being won in Jesus Christ, but which must also go on as long as the history of the human race goes on. This victory is first and foremost a communion with God (who knows us by name . . .) It is also the participation in his own glory . . . It is deliverance . . . and finally, it is the mysterious promise of everlasting life.

4. *An Evening Prayer*—Psalm 91 is traditionally used for the Compline service. It is indeed a beautiful prayer for the end of the day, to prepare ourselves to rest "in the shade of the Almighty," to be delivered from "the terror of the night" and "the plague that prowls in the darkness." It can prepare us for a truly relaxing sleep, for in it we ask God for peace, tranquility and hope.

How many of us let our evenings be poisoned with the cares and anxieties of the day which, entering our subconscious, will later disturb our sleep? Let us instead trust in God and tell him: "You are my refuge and my stronghold . . . I trust in you . . . your faithfulness is my shield . . . You will conceal me under your wings . . . No evil can fall upon me, O Lord . . . for you are with me!"

PSALM 92

טוֹב לְהֹדוֹת לַיהוָה

YOUR DEEDS HAVE MADE ME GLAD

2 It is good to give thanks to the Lord
to make music to your name, O Most High,
3 to proclaim your love in the morning
and your truth in the watches of the night,
4 on the ten-stringed lyre and the lute,
with the murmuring sound of the harp.

5 Your deeds, O Lord, have made me glad;
for the works of your hands I shout with joy.
6 O Lord, how great are your works!
How deep are your designs!
7 The foolish man cannot know this
and the fool cannot understand.

8 Though the wicked spring up like grass
and all who do evil thrive:
they are doomed to be eternally destroyed.
9 But you, Lord, are eternally on high.
10 See how your enemies perish;
all doers of evil are scattered.

11 To me you give the wild-ox's strength;
you anoint me with the purest oil.
12 My eyes look in triumph on my foes;
my ears hear gladly of their fall.
13 The just will flourish like the palm-tree
and grow like the Lebanon cedar.

14 Planted in the house of the Lord
they will flourish in the courts of our God,

15 still bearing fruit when they are old,
      still full of sap, still green,
16 to proclaim that the Lord is just.
      In him, my rock, there is no wrong.

■

HOW GOOD IT IS
   —to give thanks . . .
   —to sing . . .
   —to proclaim . . .

THE LOVE AND THE FAITHFULNESS of God who
manifested himself through his glorious deeds

THE WICKED
   —do not understand.
   —They seem to succeed, but they are doomed to complete
   annihilation
   You alone, Lord, are eternal.

THE JUST
   —in contrast are strength
                     lucidity
                     vitality
                     growth
                     fecundity

   because they lean on the Rock in which
   "there is no wrong."

■

A FIRST READING: WITH ISRAEL

This psalm is very similar to Psalm 1: a righteous man sings his happiness which stems from contemplating without ceasing the Lord's deeds, the works of his love, of his *hesed*. He witnesses the evanescence of the wicked whose success is fragile and short-lived while the just flourish in God's strength.

The Book of Job realistically acknowledged that the wicked sometimes seem to enjoy complete prosperity on this earth while the just seem to experience failure. The Book of Wisdom gave us a definitive explanation: "The souls of the upright are in the hands of God and no torment can touch them. To the unenlightened, they appeared to die . . . but they are at peace. If, as it seemed to us, they suffered punishment, their hope was rich with immortality . . . But the godless will be duly punished for their reasoning" (Wis 3:1–10).

A SECOND READING: WITH JESUS

Jesus, more than anybody else, was this "just man" who was steeped in an atmosphere of thanksgiving to the Father, night and day, and who was "planted in the house of the Lord."

Just as in this psalm, he compared himself to a tree, verdant, and full of sap: "I am the vine, you are the branches. Whoever remains in me, with me in him, bears fruit in plenty" (Jn 15:5). After the apparent failure of the cross, the resurrection served as proof of the prophetic accuracy of this psalm and Jesus is still "bearing fruit" two thousand years after his death.

As for the defeat of God's enemies, Jesus also told us that it was an inescapable fact. Even as he stood in front of the tribunal that was to condemn him, he proclaimed God's final victory: "I tell you that from this time onward you will see the Son of man seated at the right hand of the Power and coming on the clouds of heaven" (Mt 26:24).

A THIRD READING: WITH OUR TIME

1. *Yearning for Happiness and Joy*—Our world is more than ever yearning for happiness, and the progress of science has

contributed to make life more pleasant. This development follows God's fundamental plan for us, for he intended his creation to be good: "God saw that it was good" (Gn 1). However, this increased prosperity of our modern world does not solve everything. Jesus reminded us that the source of true happiness lies not in material goods (Lk 12:15). Moreover, prosperity is not evenly distributed and this is why Jesus stressed that we must share in a more equitable fashion.

And finally, in spite of our material well-being, we should always keep in mind that we are mortal and that lasting happiness can be found only in the Eternal One.

2. *"The Wicked Spring Up Like Grass and All Who Do Evil Thrive"*—Today, some pessimists claim that there has never been such moral and religious decadence as there is now, but at the time of the psalmist, Israel was a tiny minority surrounded by an ocean of paganism. Today, as in those times, we must hang onto our faith and to its rules of conduct, even if this means going against the current, and the fact that atheism seems to be winning should only be one more incentive for us to believe.

3. *"The Foolish Man Cannot Know This and the Fool Cannot Understand"*—The Bible constantly calls "fools" those who look only at superficial appearances and are impressed by the ephemeral success of the wicked. Our faith is wisdom, and it invites us to go beyond appearances and to delve into the deeper significance of things.

PSALM 95

לְכוּ נְרַנְּנָה לַיהֹוָה

O THAT TODAY YOU WOULD LISTEN TO HIS VOICE!

1 Come, ring out our joy to the Lord;
  hail the rock who saves us.
2 Let us come before him, giving thanks,
  with songs let us hail the Lord.

3 A mighty God is the Lord,
  a great king above all gods.
4 In his hands are the depths of the earth;
  the heights of the mountains are his.
5 To him belongs the sea, for he made it
  and the dry land shaped by his hands.

6 Come in; let us bow and bend low;
  let us kneel before the God who made us
7 For he is our God and we
  the people who belong to his pasture,
  the flock that is led by his hand.

  O that to-day you would listen to his voice!
8 Harden not your hearts as at Meribah,
  as on that day at Massah in the desert
9 when your fathers put me to the test;
  when they tried me, though they saw my work.

10 For forty years I was wearied of this generation*
  and I said: "Their hearts are astray,
  these people do not know my ways."

---

* For v. 10, the Grail version reads: "these people" instead of "this genera-tion."

154

11 Then I took an oath in my anger:
   "Never shall they enter my rest."

■

FIRST INVITATION:
   Come,
   ring out your joy,
   give thanks,
   hail.
   GOD, CREATOR AND MASTER OF THE UNIVERSE
   the earth,
   the mountains,
   the sea.

SECOND INVITATION:
   Come,
   bow and bend low,
   adore.
   GOD, THE SHEPHERD WHO LEADS HISTORY
   Divine oracle recalling former infidelities
   But *today* will we listen to his word,
   and follow the path
   that will lead us to rest?

■

A FIRST READING: WITH ISRAEL

This psalm, with which religious men and women and priests start their day, was also used by the Jews in the ceremonies of the renewal of the Covenant. Twice, the Levites, who were the Masters of Ceremonies for religious events, would invite the congregation to take an active part in the celebration: "Come, acclaim, shout . . . enter, bow and bend low!" To each invitation the crowd would respond with a ritual formula: "A mighty God is the Lord (Creation). . . . He is our God (Covenant)."

We then hear a sort of oracle: God speaks to remind his people of the importance of the Covenant, of its historic dimension and of its value for today.

A SECOND READING: WITH JESUS

Jesus wanted to experience personally a time in the desert, the place of testing, the place of temptation and of challenge to God—at Meribah and Massah—(Ex 17:1–7; Nb 20:1–13). During forty days, reminiscent of the forty years of the long trial of the desert, Jesus was tempted. And his temptation took on precisely the same form as it did for the people of Israel: (1) the temptation of hunger, (2) the temptation of idolatry and (3) the temptation of miraculous signs.

"For forty years I was wearied of this generation." The word "generation" is used here in a pejorative manner, and Jesus himself used it several times in this way: "Why does this generation demand a sign? . . . No sign shall be given to this generation" (Mk 8:12).—"It is an evil and unfaithful generation that asks for a sign" (Mt 12:39).—"Faithless generation, how much longer must I be among you? (Mk 9:19)

"The flock that is led by his hand"—Jesus used this theme of the shepherd: "I am the Good Shepherd" (Jn 10).—"When he saw the crowds he felt sorry for them because they were . . . like sheep without a shepherd" (Mt 9:36).

We also have the metaphor of the rock: "Everyone who listens to these words of mine and acts on them will be like a sensible man who built his house on rock" (Mt 7:24).

A THIRD READING: WITH OUR TIME

1. *An Invitation: Come In! Let Us Shout with Joy! Let Us Praise!* —"No man is an island." The impersonal climate of big cities is the source of a loneliness which makes us want to be with others. Today, our liturgy is trying to stress the value of community participation—a value we should never have forgotten! If the church asks us to gather together in the same place and at the same time, it is not for individual prayer, but to pray *together*: "Come, shout with joy! Sing and praise!"

2. *The Covenant—"He Is Our God, We Are His People."— Are We Willing to Listen to Him?*—"Covenant" is the key word of the Bible, an extraordinary adventure for God who unites himself—in love—with his people, with mere human beings. This sheds light on the union of matrimony and makes it a "sacrament of faith." The essential elements of human love are also the essential elements of faith.

3. *Sin Is A Breach of Faithfulness and A Refusal to Listen*— We are struck by the reproachful tone at the end of this psalm: it has the ring of "injured love." Such is indeed the true dimension of sin, and we tremendously water down evil when we look at it only as the transgression of a law. Sin does much more than that: it disappoints God, it hurts him. Instead of accusing or challenging God because of the presence of evil in the world, we should understand that evil is contrary to the plan of God. It is God who is the first one to suffer from evil, like an artist who witnesses the destruction of his masterpiece or like a lover whose love has been rejected.

4. *Today*—It is not by chance that the church suggests that we pray this psalm every morning. The invitation to joyful praise expressed in the beginning of this hymn is a daily invitation. And even the severe admonition to resist temptation is also a positive invitation. Today everything is possible. The past is the past and yesterday's sins are over. A new day is beginning.

PSALM 96　　שִׁירוּ לַיהוָה שִׁיר חָדָשׁ

HE COMES TO RULE THE EARTH

1 O sing a new song to the Lord,
　 sing to the Lord all the earth.
2 O sing to the Lord, bless his name.

　 Proclaim his help day by day,
3 tell among the nations his glory
　 and his wonders among the peoples.

4 The Lord is great and worthy of praise,
　 to be feared above all gods;
5 the gods of the heathens are naught.

　 It was the Lord who made the heavens,
6 his are majesty and state and power
　 and splendour in his holy place.

7 Give the Lord, you families of peoples,
　 give the Lord glory and power,
8 give the Lord the glory of his name.

　 Bring an offering and enter his courts,
9 worship the Lord in his temple.
　 O earth, tremble before him.

10 Proclaim to the nations: "God is king."
　 The world he made firm in its place;
　 he will judge the people in fairness.

11 Let the heavens rejoice and earth be glad,
　 let the sea and all within it thunder praise,
12 let the land and all it bears rejoice,
　 all of the trees of the wood shout for joy

13   at the presence of the Lord for he comes,
he comes to rule the earth.
With justice he will rule the world,
he will judge the peoples with his truth.

■

Sing!
Sing!
Do Sing!

ISRAEL AMIDST THE NATIONS . . .

proclaims the Good News of the Lord

—**great**
—**worthy of praise**
—**the Creator**
—**splendor**
—**majesty**
—**power and beauty**

AND ALL THE NATIONS THEMSELVES . . .
—**glory and power**
—**holiness**
—**king**
—**justice**

AND THE ENTIRE COSMOS . . .
—**the heavens**
—**the earth**
—**the sea**
—**the land**
—**the trees**

FOR HE IS COMING!
—**justice**
—**truth**

■

A FIRST READING: WITH ISRAEL

This psalm, used during the midnight mass of Christmas emphatically urges us "to sing." The word *sing* is repeated three times in the first three lines. Further on, we have the same urging, three more times: "Give the Lord glory! Give the Lord glory! Do give him glory!"

Who then is invited to this celebration? First the people of God, Israel, and also the New Israel. But the believers are not allowed to keep the Good News of salvation to themselves. Christmas must be celebrated with everybody: we must proclaim his glory to the pagan nations and his wonders to all the peoples. The church—the people of God's praise—must be a missionary church whose mission it is to invite every man and woman to God's feast, to a universal feast, a truly "catholic" celebration.

Israel is not the only nation in charge of praising: all the "families of peoples" are also summoned to the temple to "bring an offering and enter his courts." God's sanctuary is open to all, not only to the believers and the righteous. Special privileges have been abolished! The Lord "is coming" for everybody. In his exaltation, the inspired psalmist who just invited Israel and all of humankind, now decides to invite nature and the cosmos: heaven and earth, the land and the sea, the trees. He lets his voice unfurl a mini-theodicy, a sort of love litany of God's attributes: "He is great, unique (the other gods are naught), the Creator: splendid, majestic, powerful, glorious, mighty, holy; he is the King, just and trustworthy.

A SECOND READING: WITH JESUS

We must reread this psalm as a prayer which has the same significance as the Lord's Prayer: *Thy Kingdom Come!* This was the prayer of Jesus . . . O Master, teach us how to pray!

We must reread this psalm with the missionary spirit of Jesus: *"Go, make disciples of all nations"* (Mt 28:19); *"Go out to the whole world; proclaim the gospel to all creation"* (Mk 16:15–16). Do not keep the Good News to yourself: "Preaching the gospel gives me nothing to boast of, for I am under compulsion and I should be in trouble if I failed to do it" (1 Co 9:16).

We must reread this psalm with the angels of Christmas who were singing in the night: "Glory to God, Peace to all!" We must sing with them: "Let the heavens rejoice and earth be glad!"

We must reread this psalm with Jesus who said he was a king. To Pilate's question: "Are you the King of the Jews?" Jesus replied, "It is you who say it" (Mt 27:12). Yes, we shall "see the Son of man coming on the clouds of heaven with power and great glory!" (Mt 24:30).

Let us rejoice for our Lord is coming!

A THIRD READING: WITH OUR TIME

1. *"Give Glory to God! Adore God! The Lord Is King!"*—May we never forget this attitude when we pray: Adoration and a sense of awe are the basis of the approach to God. God is the *All-Other,* the Transcendent One, who stands far beyond our grasp. But the revelation of the closeness of God who became one of us, who became a little child at Christmas, does not take anything away from this feeling of adoration. Paradoxically, God's infinitude shines out even in this exorbitant love which made him come into our world—in a manger intended for animals!

2. *"The Gods of the Heathens Are Naught . . . It Is Our Lord Who Made the Heavens"*—Let us accept from the Jewish tradition this lesson in uncompromising monotheism. Only God is God! Everything else we may be tempted to worship, be it the stars or the sky, money or power . . . has been created by God, but they are not God and when we adore them we become their slaves. There is something eminently freeing in the affirmation of the uniqueness of God: There is no other absolute, no other God.

3. *"Day By Day, Proclaim the Good News of His Salvation and His Wondrous Deeds to All the Peoples . . ."*—The psalmist invites us to enthusiastically share the Good News throughout *space* (all the earth, all men and women, all cultures) and through *time* (day by day). Are we "spreaders" of the Good News? And if we are too shy to proclaim it, is it perhaps that we ourselves have not experienced it as "good?" In this case, it is better to remain silent! If we perceive our Christian faith as only

a moral code, a duty or a constraint, then please, let us not even talk about it! But if we perceive it as "Good News," then, by all means, let us shout it from the mountain tops!

4. "*The Heavens Rejoice, the Earth Exults, the Sea Thunders Praise, the Land Rejoices, the Trees Shout for Joy . . .*"—This abundance of joyful expressions should be for us an invitation to joy. According to Thomas Aquinas, "sadness is a sin!" And indeed continuous gloominess, a cantankerous mood or a grumpy face are insults to God.

Smiling is one of the first expressions of love.

PSALM 97

יְהוָה מָלָךְ תָּגֵל הָאָרֶץ

THE LORD MOST HIGH ABOVE ALL THE EARTH

1 The Lord is king, let earth rejoice,
let all the coastlands be glad.
2 Clouds and darkness are his raiment;
his throne, justice and right.

3 A fire prepares his path;
it burns up his foes on every side.
4 His lightnings light up the world,
the earth trembles at the sight.

5 The mountains melt like wax
before the Lord of all the earth.
6 The skies proclaim his justice;
all peoples see his glory.

7 Let those who serve idols be ashamed,
those who boast of their worthless gods.
All you spirits, worship him.

8 Zion hears and is glad;
the people of Judah rejoice
because of your judgements O Lord.

9 For you indeed are the Lord
most high above all the earth
exalted far above all spirits.

10 The Lord loves those who hate evil:
he guards the souls of his saints;
he sets them free from the wicked.

11   Light is sown for the just*
     and joy for the upright of heart.
12   Rejoice, you just, in the Lord;
     give glory to his holy name.

■

THE LORD IS KING . . .
A majestic theophany, like the one on Mount Sinai:
—**clouds**
—**darkness**
—**fire**
—**lightning**
—**earthquakes**

THE LORD OF ALL THE EARTH . . .
—**justice**
—**glory**
in front of *him*,
idols are worthlessness . . .
          vanity . . .
the faithful are feast . . .
               joy . . .
under one condition: they must hate evil
   light . . .
   joy . . .
   eucharist . . .

■

---

* For v. 11 the Grail version reads:
"Light shines forth from the just."

A FIRST READING: WITH ISRAEL

This is a "Psalm of Kingship." Once more Israel invites all the earth to come to a festival celebrating the kingship of God.

The greatness of God is proclaimed in all of his titles: "Yahweh is King, the Lord of all the earth, the Lord Most High above all the earth, His Holy Name . . ." As on Mount Sinai the majesty of God is revealed in a theophany: storm, clouds and darkness, fire and lightning, the mountains "melt like wax," "the earth trembles."

This concrete revelation of God who appears amidst cosmic forces which are out of man's control gives rise to two antithetical results:

—the false gods, the idols, everything that is vain and meaningless, disappears in the face of the true and only God. An uncompromising monotheism orders all the false gods to fall on their knees: "all you spirits, worship him!"

—the faithful of God, on the other hand, the just, the *hasidim,* experience joy and happiness but under one condition: they must "hate evil." The religion of Israel is not a religion of half-measures or of watered-down attitudes. One must choose: "Let those who serve idols be ashamed."

A SECOND READING: WITH JESUS

"The Lord is King!"—"Thy Kingdom come on earth as it is in heaven." Jesus' entire life was passionately devoted to his Father's kingdom. Yet, although Jesus was the Son of God, he deliberately avoided any ostentatious display of divine power during the time of his incarnation. He systematically refused those theophanies which the Jews of his time were so fond of. When they asked "if he would show them a sign from heaven," Jesus replied: "the only sign you will be given is the sign of Jonah. And he left them and went off" (Mt 16:1–4).

Compared to the Old Testament, the New Testament is very discreet. Only once, during the transfiguration, is a theophany recorded: "a bright cloud covered them with shadow" (Mt 17:5).

Jesus used this same biblical language when he announced

his glory to come in front of the Sanhedrin: "You will see the Son of man . . . coming on the clouds of heaven" (Mt 26:64; Rv 1:7).

The author of the Letter to the Hebrews quoted this psalm when he compared the incarnation to the enthronement of a king: "When he brings the First-born into the world, he says: Let all the angels of God pay him homage" (Hb 1:6).

But above all, it is the Parousia of Jesus, his return in glory, which should be compared to this psalm: "The coming of the Son of man will be like lightning striking in the east and flashing far into the west . . ." (Mt 24:27).

At that time, the righteous will be associated with this triumph, as the psalmist tells us and as the author of the Letter to the Colossians reminds us in a powerful way: "Fortified in accordance with his glorious strength, giving thanks with joy to the Father who has made you able to share the lot of God's holy people and with them to inherit the light . . . he has rescued us from the ruling force of darkness and transferred us to the kingdom of the Son that he loves" (Col 1:11–12).

Finally, when the Holy Spirit came down at Pentecost, there was also storm and fire.

A THIRD READING: WITH OUR TIME

1. *Before God*—Truly alive is the God before whom I stand! Five times in the psalm we are invited to stand "before" God, and this is very significant. Men and women do not really have an autonomous existence: their being cannot stand on its own . . . they can only be "before" God, for God *is*. We, on the other hand can only *be* "before" him.

2. *Fire As A Symbol of God*—"A fire prepares his path; it burns up his foes on every side. His lightnings light up the world . . . the mountains melt like wax before the Lord. . . ." We men and women of the twentieth century would be ill-advised to dismiss these images as childish. It is true that they conjure up some of the ancient myths, like that of Prometheus who was defeated as he tried to master the fire of the gods. Although modern science has taught us how to harness fire to some degree, more importantly it has taught us that we live on "cyclones of fire." The core of the earth is a formidable fire which some-

times erupts through volcanoes. The universe is a fantastic collection of fireballs—the stars. Our sun is nothing but a gigantic and continuing atomic explosion, which no one will ever be able to approach without being "burnt up," as the psalmist tells us. In the midst of this grandiose and terrifying universe, the hand of the Creator has reserved a warm place where human life can flourish, the planet Earth. He limited our existence to a certain time and a certain place.

3. *"Hate Evil"*—Our modern society makes constant use of the language of battle; so did the Bible! This psalm is not a relaxing psalm; it urges us to fight against evil, to set ourselves free from the powers of evil, with the help of God.

4. *"Light Is Sown for the Just and Joy for the Upright of Heart."*—The image of the planting season softens the violence of the other images. Rather than blazing flashes of lightning, the kingdom of God is a seed which has been sown and will slowly grow. The light and the joy of God which have been sown amidst the human race will grow little by little. We must believe it! Israel, which was at the mercy of the surrounding pagan nations, kept on believing that "a light had been sown."

PSALM 98 שִׁירוּ לַיהוה שִׁיר חָדָשׁ

ALL THE EARTH HAS SEEN THE SALVATION OF OUR GOD

1 Sing a new song to the Lord
for he has worked wonders.
His right hand and holy arm
have brought salvation.

2 The Lord has made known his salvation;
has shown his justice to the nations.
3 He has remembered his truth and love
for the house of Israel.

All the ends of the earth have seen
the salvation of our God.
4 Shout to the Lord all the earth,
ring out your joy.

5 Sing psalms to the Lord with the harp
with the sound of music.
6 With the trumpet and the sound of the horn
acclaim the King, the Lord.

* * *

7 Let the sea and all within it, thunder;
the world, and all its peoples.
8 Let the rivers clap their hands
and the hills ring out their joy

9 at the presence of the Lord: for he comes,
he comes to rule the earth.
He will rule the world with justice
and the peoples with fairness.

■

GOD'S DEEDS:
   —He has worked wonders . . .
   —He has brought salvation . . .
   —He has shown his justice . . .
   —He has remembered his "faithful love" (*hesed*)

THE RESPONSE OF THE UNIVERSE:
   —Acclaim . . .
   —Shout, sing, play . . .
   —on all the instruments . . .

   —Let the sea thunder . . .
   —all men and women . . .
   —Let the rivers clap their hands . . .
   —Let the hills ring out their joy . . .

HE IS COMING . . .
   —He will rule the world with "justice" and "fairness."

■

A FIRST READING: WITH ISRAEL

This is one of the "Psalms of Kingship." Once a year, during the Festival of the Tabernacles (reminiscent of the forty years Israel spent in the desert) Jerusalem would celebrate her king with a huge popular festival. Astoundingly enough, this "king" they were celebrating was not a man (no longer a man since the Davidic dynasty had long died out) but was Yahweh himself. Psalm 98 is an invitation to this festival, which climaxed in a gigantic royal acclamation: "Our God reigns! Shout to the Lord your King!" Let us try to imagine this *terouah* (there is no English translation for this word which means "shout," "ovation," and "acclamation"). It was originally a war cry when Yahweh led the armies of Israel to victory. Here it is a general rejoicing, shouts of joy while the bright trumpets and the raucous horns resound amidst the clappings of hands of the exalted crowd.

Why this joy? Six verbs explain it to us: it is because of six of God's deeds. Five of them are expressed in the past tense: "He has worked wonders . . . his right hand has brought salvation . . . he has made known his salvation . . . he has remembered his *hesed*. . . . He has come." At the end, there is one verb in the future: "He will rule the world with justice and the peoples with fairness."

Note the universalism of Hebrew thought: *Salvation* (justice-faithfulness-love), with which Israel has been gifted is, in fact, intended for all nations, and her God, whom she acclaims as her only king, shall one day rule over the whole world. No wonder then that she shouts with all her might to celebrate him! No wonder that the seas, the rivers the mountains, and all of nature "clap their hands for joy!"

A SECOND READING: WITH JESUS

Now that we have read this psalm in its literal meaning—as Israel would have read it, we must reread it in the light of the "Jesus-event"—we must even say it in the name of Jesus, in union with his feelings and his prayer when he applied it to his role in God's plan.

1. *The "Advent" of God*—Israel had no idea how true this would become, and this hymn actually sings of Christmas, of the coming of the Son of God himself. This is why the church uses it during mass on Christmas Day while she uses a very similar psalm (96) during Midnight Mass.

2. *The Revelation of God's Faithful Love*—The incarnation of the Word is the historical event which makes visible, which "lifts the veil" (this is the meaning of the word "revelation") on the love God gives to Israel and then extends to all the peoples, through Jesus . . .

3. *The New Covenant—The New Liberation*—It is fitting to sing "a new song" for God renews his Covenant, and the celebration of the "advent" of God is a sign, a sacrament which gives it its full meaning. When we acclaim God as king, we do not actually confer kingship upon him—since he has been king for ever—we actualize this kingship and we anticipate the Second Coming. When we celebrate Christmas, we truly "make God come" in a real, sacramental way.

4. *Salvation*—Simeon exulted: "My eyes have seen the salvation which you have made ready in the sight of the nations" (Lk 2:30). As he neared his Passover, Jesus exulted: "I shall draw all people to myself" (Jn 12:32). And the evangelist exulted: "Jesus was to die for the nation—and not for the nation only, but also to gather together into one the scattered children of God" (Jn 11:52). And this great and universal vision actualized in Christ had been foretold by the hope of an entire nation who had dared to invite all the earth, all the nations, all men and women to celebrate their own *terouah*—a truly universal festival! We are on the way to a feast where all men and women will be happy together and celebrate together on the same day the same God and the same Love who saved them!

A THIRD READING: WITH OUR TIME

1. *Let Us Celebrate!*—Let us not procrastinate, let us respond to the invitation! Let us go! Let us prepare our musical instruments, our voices, and our hand clappings. . . . Why is it that some people are shocked by the noise young people of *today* make

when they celebrate? There is, of course, a time for silent prayer, for intimate prayer, but there is also a time for loud, joyful prayer.

2. *He Will Rule the World with Justice*—Justice! A world ruled with justice, according to God! This *will* happen! A world ruled according to Love . . . This *is* happening . . . The Lord is coming. The kingdom of God is already happening!

PSALM 100

הָרִיעוּ לַיהוָה כָּל־הָאָרֶץ

GIVE THANKS TO THE LORD: HE IS FAITHFUL

1 Cry out with joy to the Lord, all the earth.
2 Serve the Lord with gladness.
Come before him, singing for joy.

3 Know that he, the Lord is God.
He made us, we belong to him,
we are his people, the sheep of his flock.

4 Go within his gates, giving thanks.
Enter his courts with songs of praise.
Give thanks to him and bless his name.

5 Indeed, how good is the Lord,
eternal his merciful love.
He is faithful from age to age.

■

SEVEN INVITATIONS:

Cry out to the Lord . . .
Serve him . . .   **gladness . . .**
Come before him . . .   **joy . . .**
Know . . .
Go to his house . . .   **thanks . . .**
Enter his courts . . .   **praises . . .**
Give thanks . . .

Why?   —because God is God
            —because he made us
            —because he is good
            —because his *love* is eternal.

■

A FIRST READING: WITH ISRAEL

Psalm 100 was used during the Ritual of the Covenant Renewal. The Bible records many instances in which Israel recelebrated the Covenant: every time a new event made them experience God's protection, or every time they had been unfaithful to the Covenant. The Covenant is the core of Israel's faith: God is our ally, he is with us, he espoused us, he linked his destiny to ours, he loves us! In spite of some biblical expressions which could lead us to believe otherwise, Israel never felt that this fantastic happiness, this amazing conviction, was an exclusive privilege. We have here an explicit invitation extended to all men and women, to all the earth, to come and share in Israel's joy and thanksgiving. The people of Israel tell us that what we already have and what we already live, the joys that fill us, are the foreshadowing of what is intended for all the earth, for all of humankind! Come, one and all! God's Covenant is with us, God's love for us is for all men and women!

A SECOND READING: WITH JESUS

Let us imagine this psalm on Jesus' lips as he sang it in Nazareth, or after talking to the crowds about his Father: "Cry out with joy to the Lord, all the earth, serve the Lord with gladness, come before him, singing for joy . . . Indeed, how good is the Lord, eternal his merciful love. He is faithful from age to age."

"I am the good shepherd: I know my own and my own know me, just as the Father knows me and I know the Father . . ." (Jn 110:14–15).

"Everlasting is his love."—"Here is the blood of the new and everlasting Covenant . . ."

"He made us, we belong to him."—"No (sparrow) falls to the ground without your Father knowing . . . so there is no need to be afraid" (Mt 10:29).

Do listen to Jesus praying this psalm, within your hearts, where his Spirit "prays within you" (Rm 8:26–31). Every mass is a reenactment of this psalm, and every liturgy is a foreshadowing of heaven . . . where all men and women will sing praises and will acknowledge that "the Lord is God!"

A THIRD READING: WITH OUR TIME

1. *Joy—Singing*—In the days of old, men and women had to bear only their own suffering and that of their family and neighborhood, maybe of their nation. Nowadays, thanks to modern media we carry the weight of the world upon our shoulders. Hence the gloominess and even the despair that sometimes overwhelms many of us.

In this context, let us listen again to the seven "commands" of this psalm: *Cry Out with joy* . . . *Serve* God with gladness . . . *Come* before him singing for joy . . . *Know* that he is God . . ., *Go* within his gates, giving thanks . . . *Enter* his courts with songs of praise . . . *Bless* his name!"—"Indeed how good is the Lord, eternal his merciful love."

2. *Joy Is Contagious*—"Know that he, the Lord is God." This awareness comes from within, freely and without any pressure. But those of us who "know" should give thanks and be happy; our happiness should be heard and seen! Do our liturgies reflect this joyous attitude? Do our lives as Christian men and women reflect the happiness we experience in our God?

3. *Why Should We Be Happy?*—Because God is God and he made us. This is God's first gift to us: our life, our existence, our being. This is his first grace, his first universal Covenant!

PSALM 103

בָּרְכִי נַפְשִׁי אֶת־יְהוָה

GOD'S LOVE FOR HIS CHILDREN

1 My soul, give thanks to the Lord,
 all my being, bless his holy name.
2 My soul, give thanks to the Lord
 and never forget all his blessings.

3 It is he who forgives all your guilt,
 who heals every one of your ills,
4 who redeems your life from the grave,
 who crowns you with love and tenderness,*
5 who fills your life with good things,
 renewing your youth like an eagle's.

6 The Lord does deeds of justice,
 gives judgement for all who are oppressed.
7 He made known his ways to Moses
 and his deeds to Israel's sons.

8 The Lord is tenderness and love,*
 slow to anger and rich to mercy.
9 His wrath will come to an end;
 he will not be angry for ever.
10 He does not treat us according to our sins
 nor repay us according to our faults.

11 For as the heavens are high above the earth
 so strong is his love for those who fear him.
12 As far as the east is from the west
 so far does he remove our sins.

---

*For vv. 4, 8, and 13 the Grail version reads "compassion" instead of "tenderness."

13   As a father has tenderness for his son,*
      the Lord has pity on those who fear him;
14   for he knows of what we are made,
      he remembers that we are dust.

15   As for man, his days are like the grass;
      he flowers like the flower of the field;
16   the wind blows and he is gone
      and his place never sees him again.

17   But the love of the Lord is from always to always†
      upon those who hold him in fear;
      his justice reaches out to children's children
18   when they keep his covenant in truth,
      when they keep his will in their mind.

19   The Lord has set his sway in heaven
      and his kingdom is ruling over all.
20   Give thanks to the Lord, all his angels,
      mighty in power, fulfilling his word,
      who heed the voice of his word.

21   Give thanks to the Lord, all his hosts,
      his servants who do his will.
22   Give thanks to the Lord, all his works,
      in every place where he rules.
      My soul, give thanks to the Lord!

■

HYMN TO THE LOVE OF GOD—THANKSGIVING
He forgives us . . .
He heals us . . .
He redeems our life . . .
He loves us tenderly . . .

---

† For v. 17 the Grail version reads "the love of the Lord is everlasting."

He fulfills us . . .

He restores youth . . .

He does "deeds of justice . . ."
He defends the oppressed . . .
He reveals himself . . .
He intervenes on behalf of his people . . .

He is full of tenderness . . .
He loves us . . .
He does not hold grudges . . .
He forgets our offences . . .
He pardons us . . .
He does not punish us according to our sins . . .

   An image: His *love* is as vast as the horizon, it extends
          from East to West.

He is our father . . .

   An image: He knows that we are weak . . .
          that we are dust . . .
          as fragile as flowers . . .

But *his love* is everlasting.

Should we not try to love him more, to obey him more?

He is the KING of the Universe.
   —Bless Yahweh, all his angels!
   —Bless Yahweh, all the cosmos!
   —Bless Yahweh, all his creation!
   —And you, my soul, bless Yahweh!

■

A FIRST READING: WITH ISRAEL

A forgiven sinner goes up to the temple to offer a sacrifice of thanksgiving during which he gives an account of the blessings he has received. He invites the crowd of family and friends that accompanies him to take part in the sacrificial banquet, to associate themselves with his thanksgiving. This is a hymn to the love of God, the God of the Covenant. Note the shift of pronouns, from the singular "I" to the plural "we." It is the whole nation of Israel that speaks through this sinner. The remission of sins was therefore not an individual but a communal act. What a profound realization of the solidarity of each sinner with all other sinners, with the sin of the world!

Too often the Old and the New Testaments have been seen in opposition, as if the former were a religion of fear and the latter a religion of love . . . Please count how many times the words *love* (*hesed*) and *tenderness* are used in this psalm! Such is our God: Tenderness and Love! The true God does not resemble at all the image the pagans had of him—that of an angry judge. Not at all! Please read this psalm again!

A SECOND READING: WITH JESUS

God is good! God is Love! God is our Father!—Jesus echoed the very words of this psalm: "as a father feels tenderness for his children . . ."—"Our Father who art in heaven forgive us our trespasses."

The result of this love is *pardon*. We can already hear the Father of the prodigal son (Lk 15:1–32). We can already hear these words: "Love your enemies . . . (then) you will have a great reward, and you will be children of the Most High, for he himself is kind to the ungrateful and the wicked" (Lk 6:27–38).

A THIRD READING: WITH OUR TIME

1. *Joy*—Joy is bursting forth in this song. Let us follow this joyful outburst which invites all the angels and the entire cosmos to join in a prayer of thanksgiving. How great are human beings! Through our souls, our "spiritual being" and our bodies we are

microcosms which sum up all of creation. "Bless the Lord, O my soul!" At the very moment I go into prayer, the entire universe sings in and through me. How great are we, human beings; we are the "chorus" of the universe! And yet *we are so fragile!* This is a truly modern thought, already expressed here in this unforgettable metaphor: "As for man, his days are like the grass; he flowers like the flower of the field; the wind blows and he is gone . . ." and then this heart-rending poetic touch: "and his place never sees him again!"

2. *Merciful Love*—There is a "motherly" quality to this love that continuously brings forth life . . . like a fantastic life-giving womb.

3. *Eternal Love*—"from always to always"—What an amazing formula! This is the true source of our belief in the resurrection.

4. *Strong Love, Powerful Love*—A love stronger than death . . . which is able to not only create but re-create us!

5. *Love Freely Accepted*—The submission God expects from us is not that of a trembling slave, but that of a joyful child.

PSALM 104   בָּרְכִי נַפְשִׁי אֶת־יְהֹוָה

HOW MANY ARE YOUR WORKS, O LORD!

1 Bless the Lord, my soul!
    Lord God, how great you are,
    clothed in majesty and glory,
2 wrapped in light as in a robe!

                    *   *   *

    You stretch out the heavens like a tent.
3 Above the rains you build your dwelling.
    You make the clouds your chariot,
    you walk on the wings of the wind,
4 you make the winds your messengers
    and flashing fire your servants.

5 You founded the earth on its base,
    to stand firm from age to age.
6 You wrapped it with the ocean like a cloak:
    the waters stood higher than the mountains.

7 At your threat they took flight;
    at the voice of your thunder they fled.
8 They rose over the mountains and flowed down
    to the place which you had appointed.
9 You set limits they might not pass
    lest they return to cover the earth.

10 You make springs gush forth in the valleys:
     they flow in between the hills.
11 They give drink to all the beasts of the field;
     the wild-asses quench their thirst.
12 On their banks dwell the birds of heaven;
     from the branches they sing their song.

13 From your dwelling you water the hills;
    earth drinks its fill of your gift.
14 You make the grass grow for the cattle
    and the plants to serve man's needs,

    that he may bring forth bread from the earth
15 and wine to cheer man's heart;
    oil, to make his face shine
    and bread to strengthen man's heart.

16 The trees of the Lord drink their fill,
    the cedars he planted on Lebanon;
17 there the birds build their nests:
    on the tree-top the stork has her home.
18 the goats find a home on the mountains
    and the rabbits hide in the rocks.

19 You made the moon to mark the months;
    the sun knows the time for its setting.
20 When you spread the darkness it is night
    and all the beasts of the forest creep forth.
21 The young lions roar for their prey
    and ask their food from God.

22 At the rising of the sun they steal away
    and go rest in their dens.
23 Man goes forth to his work,
    to labour till evening falls.

24 How many are your works, O Lord!
    In wisdom you have made them all.
    The earth is full of your riches.

25 There is the sea, vast and wide,
    with its moving swarms past counting,
    living things great and small.
26 The ships are moving there
    and the monsters you made to play with.

27 All of these look to you
    to give them their food in due season.
28 You give it, they gather it up:
    you open your hand, they have their fill.

29 You hide your face, they are dismayed;
    you take back your spirit, they die,
    returning to the dust from which they came.
30 You send forth your spirit, they are created;
    and you renew the face of the earth.

31 May the glory of the Lord last for ever!
    May the Lord rejoice in his work!
32 He looks on the earth and it trembles;
    the mountains send forth smoke at his touch.

33 I will sing to the Lord all my life,
    make music to my God while I live.
34 May my thoughts be pleasing to him.
    I find my joy in the Lord.
35 Let sinners vanish from the earth
    and the wicked exist no more.

    Bless the Lord, my soul.

■

Hymn to the Creator

FIRST DAY: LIGHT-DARKNESS

SECOND DAY: THE FIRMAMENT
the clouds
the winds
the "flashing fire"

THIRD DAY: THE EARTH—THE WATERS
> the oceans
> the thunder
> the mountains
> the valleys
> the rivers
> the "beasts of the field"
> the wild asses
> the birds
>
> the meadows
> the fields
>
> bread
> wine
> oil
>
> the trees
> the cedars
> the storks
> the goats
> the rabbits

FOURTH DAY: THE STARS
> the moon
> the sun
>
> the forests
> the lions
>
> Man

HOW MANY ARE YOUR WORKS!

■

A FIRST READING: WITH ISRAEL

The author of this psalm has copied an Egyptian hymn in honor of Aton-Ra, god of the sun, composed by Amenophet IV, but purified it of any idolatrous ideas. He inserted his song of praise into the framework of the six days of Genesis, and put into it the same basic optimism vis-à-vis nature, as well as the same warning against the evil which human freedom can inflict upon nature, and which must at last disappear.

A SECOND READING: WITH JESUS

The fourth evangelist presented Jesus as the incarnate Word: "In the beginning was the Word: the Word was with God and the Word was God . . . Through him all things came into being, not one thing came into being except through him . . . in him was life" (Jn 1:1–3)—"And the Word was made flesh . . ." (14).

Let us for a moment imagine Jesus, the God-Man who came to live in the midst of his creation, strolling through his domain —his masterpiece—and looking at the sea and the sun, at human beings and animals.

The mention of bread and wine right in the middle of the work of human hands, reminds us of the Last Supper, when Jesus took these two elements in his hands to "re-present himself." The church uses this psalm on Pentecost because of the evocation of the *breath* of God as life-giving: "Lord, send us your Spirit to renew the face of the earth." And, on the evening of Pentecost, Jesus "breathed" on his disciples (Jn 20:22).

A THIRD READING: WITH OUR TIME

We must constantly rediscover the beauty, the fecundity and the power of creation. What a terrible shame it would be if we took for granted the mountains, the forests and the flowers without being sensitive to what they represent.

This psalm emphasizes the phenomenon of life connected with water. Science makes us more aware of biological processes, but instead of destroying our sense of wonder, it should amplify it.

Above all, let us not forget that creation is an ongoing process. God never ceases to maintain in being what already exists . . . He goes on creating right now! And Genesis tells us that God creates no longer without us, but with us. "Fill the earth and subdue it" (Gen 1:28). But the human race is capable of destroying all the wonders of creation, hence the final plea: "Let the sinners vanish from the earth and the wicked exist no more."

Christian thought is basically optimistic (creation is good and pleases God, the psalmist tells us), but it is not a naive and complacent optimism, for we know that creation can be perfected only when we fight "with God" against evil.

PSALM 110

נְאֻם יְהֹוָה לַאדֹנִי

"SIT ON MY RIGHT!"

1   The Lord's revelation to my Master:
    'Sit on my right:
    til I have made your enemies your footstool.'*

2   The Lord will wield from Zion
    your sceptre of power:
    rule in the midst of all your foes.

3   A prince from the day of your birth
    on the holy mountain;
    from the womb before the dawn I begot you.

4   The Lord has sworn an oath he will not change.
    "You are a priest for ever,
    a priest like Melchizedek of old."

                    *   *   *

5   The Master standing at your right hand
    will shatter kings in the day of his wrath.

6   He, the Judge of the nations,
    will heap high the bodies;
    heads will be shattered far and wide.

7   He shall drink from the stream by the wayside
    and therefore he shall lift up his head.

---

* For v. 1 the Grail version reads:
"your foes I will put beneath your feet."

■

Enthronement of the Messiah

KING
    —in communion with God . . .
    —victor over evil . . .
    —his power comes from God . . .
    —his "birth" is the reason for his communion with God
    and his royal dignity: He is the *Son of God*

PRIEST
    —for ever . . .
    —his origin is mysterious . . .
    —he will destroy all evil during the eschatological bat-
    tle . . .
    —he has drunk from the stream of immortality, he is in-
    vincible.

■

A FIRST READING: WITH ISRAEL

This is a "Royal Psalm" whose setting is the throne room of the royal palace at Jerusalem. The religious ceremony of the anointing takes place in the temple and is followed by the enthronement according to a precise ritual. First, a prophet invites the new king to sit on his *throne*—in the name of God. On the throne steps are sculptures of enemy warriors (lying on the ground) which the king symbolically tramples. At this point the prophet hands him his scepter and addresses him with his prestigious *title:* "You are the Son of God." The new king is then ordained a *priest* (every king in the East was also a priest whose special sacerdotal duty was to offer sacrifices). Finally, the prophet promises victories to the new king: he will be the *judge* who will destroy the wicked.

In reality, Royal Psalms were not always used for the actual investiture of a king—since the monarchy was short-lived in Israel—but in the ceremony which was a symbolic "recasting" to *recall and hope for the advent of the messiah* whom God was to send to his people. The messianic hope of Israel is expressed in this song which is so full of intensely poetic imagery.

A SECOND READING: WITH JESUS

"While the Pharisees were gathered round, Jesus put to them this question: 'What is your opinion about the Christ? Whose son is he?' They told him, 'David's.' He said to them, 'Then how is it that David, moved by the Spirit, calls him Lord, where he says:

"The Lord declared to my Lord,
take your seat at my right hand,
till I have made your enemies
your footstool?"

'If David calls him Lord, how then can he be his son?' No one could think of anything to say in reply, and from that day no one dared to ask him any further questions" (Mt 22:41–46).

Jesus was emphasizing the mysterious character of his origin and suggesting that he was the long-awaited messiah.

The psalmist did not know how accurately what he was predicting would come true:

—*Son of God* begotten in eternity . . .

—*Seated at the right of God* through his glorious Ascension . . .

—*He made his enemies his footstool,* and the last enemy to be conquered is death . . . but also sin and any "evil power."

—*King*—He is fully king but his kingdom is not of this world and we keep affirming this kingship when we pray: "through Jesus Christ, your Son, our Lord, who *reigns* with you and the Holy Spirit now and forever."

—*A Priest Forever*—A priest not of the order of Aaron (Jewish priests only performed animal sacrifices), but of the order of Melchizedek (the king-priest who offered up bread and wine). Jesus did not offer to God something external to himself: he offered his own self as a holy sacrifice: "This is my body given up for you, this is my blood poured out for you."

—*He Will Judge the Nations* on the Day of the Lord. This is the explicit affirmation of God's final and decisive victory. "When the Son of man comes in glory escorted by all the angels, then he will take his seat on his throne of glory. All nations will be assembled before him" (Mt 25:31–32).

A THIRD READING: WITH OUR TIME

1. *Jesus, My King*—Not a king in his palace, but a king in my heart and my life. "My King" does not reign like the earthly kings "who lord it over" their subjects and "make their authority felt," but in being a servant: "the Son of man came not to be served but to serve and to give his life as a ransom for many" (Mt 20:24–28). Every moment of my life I want him to reign, I want him to be the king of my heart and spirit and of my work.

2. *Jesus, My Victory*—In this world I have to face many battles and Jesus is my victory. Jesus triumphs when Justice, Love and Truth triumph because of me . . . in this world where there are so many evil forces at work.

3. *Jesus, My Eternal Priest*—During each mass I renew the offering Jesus made of himself on the cross. I take part in his wonderful sacrifice, the greatest act of service and love ever experienced in a man's heart . . . the total gift of himself which Jesus freely wanted to give. "No one can have greater love than to lay down his life for his friends . . ." (Jn 15:13). This is my priest! This is the priest I celebrate during each eucharist. He is the immortal spring from which I drink when I receive communion. He is the celebration of love, the presence of love and the source of love. I give thanks to you, my Love!

PSALM 113

הַלְלוּ אֶת־שֵׁם יְהוָה

MAY THE NAME OF THE LORD BE BLESSED!

1   Alleluia!

Praise, O servants of the Lord,
praise the name of the Lord!
2   May the name of the Lord be blessed
both now and for evermore!
3   From the rising of the sun to its setting
praised be the name of the Lord!

4   High above all the nations is the Lord,
above the heavens his glory.
5   Who is like the Lord, our God,
who has risen on high to his throne
6   yet stoops from the heights to look down,
to look down upon heaven and earth?

7   From the dust he lifts up the lowly,
from the dungheap he raises the poor
8   to set him in the company of princes,
yes, with the princes of his people.
9   To the childless wife he gives a home
and gladdens her heart with children.

■

AN INVITATION TO PRAISE THE NAME OF GOD
   —in all times . . .
   —in all places . . .

HE IS THE MOST HIGH, THE TRANSCENDENT ONE
   —"higher" than all the peoples,
   —"higher" than the heavens,

—his throne is set on high so he can see everything and judge everything.

HE LOVES THE POOR
—the poor man becomes a prince,
—the barren woman becomes fertile.

■

A FIRST READING: WITH ISRAEL

This is the opening hymn of the Hallel (Psalms 113–118), which the Jews sing during the Passover meal and at the great feasts. The first stanza, sung by the Levites, is an invitation to sing (the verb "praise" is repeated three times). The two other stanzas are the response of the congregation which praises God for two apparently contradictory reasons:

1. God is "high" above the nations.

2. He stoops down to look at the poor and he loves the weak.

In order to understand this psalm fully we must remember the biblical background: the lowly, the poor raised from the dungheap, collectively represent the people of Israel whom God literally raised from slavery to make them into a royal people. The poor barren woman is Sarah, old and childless, who was gifted with Isaac and became the mother of peoples as numerous as the stars of heaven. She is also Hannah, the sterile woman who became the happy mother of Samuel. She is finally Zion, the barren, exiled mother to whom many descendants were given (Is 49:21).

A SECOND READING: WITH JESUS

Jesus sang this very psalm on the evening of Holy Thursday. Let us try to imagine the fervor with which he must have prayed it that evening and how he must have adapted it to his own situation.

—The name of God—Jesus made it known and loved, and that very evening he rejoiced in the fact that he had revealed the Father's name: "I have revealed your name to those whom you took from the world to give me" (Jn 17:6).

—The Almighty stoops down and looks upon the earth. On Holy Thursday Jesus stooped down to wash his disciples' feet. The Word of God, the Lord and Master did not insist on his rank but went down to the dust to lift up the lowly and let them take part in the princely dignity of the Son of God.

Of course there is an amazing similarity between this psalm and Mary's Magnificat. She, too, praised the name of God; she, too, sang of the God who "lifts up the lowly," and above all she was that happy woman to whom God granted an unexpected virginal fruitfulness and whom generations would call "blessed."

How could Jesus not think of the paschal mystery when he uttered these prophetic words: "From the dust he lifts up the lowly to set him in the company of princes"? Jesus' resurrection, which he had been announcing to his disciples for several weeks, would be the fulfillment of the promise of this psalm. Thanks to Jesus, the poor were truly lifted up from the dust of death and made to sit at the right hand of the Father.

A THIRD READING: WITH OUR TIME

1. *God's Transcendence*—"Who is like the Lord, our God? His glory is high above the mountains." Nothing can be compared to God, absolutely nothing . . . he is far beyond any created category; he is of an order different from anything we can possibly imagine or experience.

2. *"Above the Heavens Is His Glory, Yet He Stoops Down From the Heights to Look Down upon Heaven and Earth"*—Modern science tells us that everything "holds together" in the universe. Every being physically depends on all the others like the works of a huge, intricate machine. The ecological movement points out the natural balances we must respect in order to survive. As for myself, at this very moment, I am but a minute fragment of a cosmos without which I cannot survive. I will die instantly if the sun no longer fulfills his role, or if there is not enough oxygen, if plants and animals cease to function normally, if thousands of my brothers and sisters stop working for me.

How could we possibly refuse to draw the obvious conclusion: This magnificent world of ours cannot possibly have been created by human hands, and it must be ruled by a Supreme Intelligence.

3. *The Lowly and the Poor*—How can we honestly pray this psalm if in our daily lives we contribute to making the living conditions of the poor worse? How can we honestly say that "God lifts up the lowly" unless we try to concretely improve the lives of the most destitute among us?

4. *Human Dignity*—"From the dust he lifts up the lowly to set him in the company of princes." Helping the poor with their material needs is not enough; we must give them back their dignity and help them to become free human beings, "princely" beings.

PSALM 116

הַאֲמַנְתִּי כִּי אֲדַבֵּר

I WILL RAISE THE CUP OF SALVATION

10 I trusted, even when I said:
     "I am sorely afflicted,"
11 and when I said in my alarm: SUFFERING
     "No man can be trusted."

12 How can I repay the Lord
     for his goodness to me?
13 The cup of salvation I will raise;   JOY
     I will call on the Lord's name.
14 My vows to the Lord I will fulfil
     before all his people.

15 It grieves the Lord
     to see his faithful die.*
16 Your servant, Lord, your servant am I;   SUFFERING
     you have loosened my bonds.

17 A thanksgiving sacrifice I make:
     I will call on the Lord's name.
18 My vows to the Lord I will fulfil   JOY
     before all his people,
19 in the courts of the house of the Lord,
     in your midst, O Jerusalem.

---

* For v. 15, the Grail version reads:
"O precious in the eyes of the Lord
is the death of his faithful."

■

FIRST STANZA: SUFFERING
Even though I was in the midst of terrible suffering and confusion which almost led me to doubt, I kept trusting in the Lord.

SECOND STANZA: JOY
"The cup of salvation I will raise."

THIRD STANZA: SUFFERING
—I believe that God will save me from death . . .
—"It grieves the Lord to see his faithful die."

FOURTH STANZA: JOY
"A thanksgiving sacrifice I make."

■

We should meditate on Psalm 116—which the church suggests we sing during mass on Holy Thursday—with special respect. We know that according to Jewish tradition, this was the fourth psalm of the Hallel or "Song of Thanksgiving" sung after the Passover meal. Jesus sang and prayed this very psalm when he instituted the sacrament of the eucharist, during the Last Supper.

A FIRST READING: WITH ISRAEL

The paschal meal, or *seder,* was—and still is—shared in every Jewish household on the first evening of Passover. On that evening, the table is beautifully set. At the end of the table, in front of the master of the house, are three pieces of matzo (the unleavened bread or "bread of affliction" which reminds us of the haste with which our ancestors left the land of their captivity). On the table are green herbs representing the fruits of the earth, and bitter herbs representing the bitterness of slavery, and of course, the roasted meat of the paschal lamb. In front of each guest, a wine cup. On four occasions during the meal, each guest drinks from the cup while saying a blessing, as a sign of happiness and gratitude toward the Lord. During the paschal meal, the youngest child asks questions to the master of the house who answers with the *Haggadah,* the story of the liberation from Egypt. At the end of the meal, everybody sings the *Hallel,* Psalms 113 to 118.

Psalm 116 sums up the feelings of the people of Israel faced with their situation at that particular time. They had been oppressed in a terrible manner, "sorely afflicted," but had finally received from Pharaoh permission to leave "the furnace." But now they are pursued by the Egyptian army ("I said in my alarm: 'no man can be trusted' ") and are experiencing human deceitfulness. They are all going to die, trapped between the Red Sea in front of them and Pharaoh's chariots behind them. This is when the Red Sea opens, for "it grieves the Lord to see his faithful die." Overwhelmed by the intensity of his feelings, the psalmist suddenly switches to the second person: "*Your* servant, Lord, *your* servant am I; *You* have loosened my bonds. A thanksgiving sacrifice I make . . ." Thus the Passover meal was (and is) a powerful expression of joy and thanksgiving toward the saving God, the one who saves us from misery and death. This is the meal Jesus experienced on that evening, the last meal he ate before dying and rising from the dead.

A SECOND READING: WITH JESUS

When he prayed this psalm with his people, Jesus gave it a new, universal dimension. The tragedy of Israel, who was oppressed and utterly miserable, is the tragedy we all face because of our human condition. Israel's prayer of gratitude "for the Lord's goodness" is that of every man and woman awaiting the promise of the resurrection.

Yes, Jesus knew he was going to die on the next day. That very evening, during the course of the meal, Judas was going to leave the group in order to initiate the final process. Yet our Lord did not allow himself to be overwhelmed by the tragedy of his human condition, but faced it freely, his head held high, and rehearsed his death. He took in his hands the "unleavened bread of affliction" set in front of him and said: "This is my body given up for you." Then he took the cup of wine and said: "This is the cup of my blood poured out for you and for many." Let us imagine Jesus—not in some abstract way, but in the context of the vigil before his own death—singing these heart-rending words: "It grieves the Lord to see his faithful die . . ." No, God does not take pleasure in death, but death is part of the human condition; it is part of "all that is not God," and is therefore inevitable. Only God is God. Only God is perfect. Only God is eternal.

Yet, what prevails in this psalm and in the heart of Jesus on that evening is *thanksgiving:* "How can I repay the Lord for his goodness to me? The cup of salvation I will raise . . . A thanksgiving sacrifice I make." How is this possible? Because Jesus had the certitude that he was loved by his father: "It grieves the Lord to see his faithful die." And Jesus knew that this love would be life-giving. God does not want death; God will save those he loves from death. Jesus did know that his death, on the next day, would not be the sinister plunge into the nothingness atheists talk about, but the entrance into "the courts of the house of the Lord," where there will be everlasting praise and thanksgiving.

A THIRD READING: WITH OUR TIME

Jesus experienced death in the same way all human beings experience it. Any ideology or conception of the human existence that neglects the evidence of death cannot pretend to be a valid ideology for humankind. Civilizations, too, are mortal! Everything we build is mortal! Everything we bring into the world is bound to die!

Today's atheist draws the inevitable, logical conclusion that the world is meaningless . . . and we add: "if God does not exist, human beings do not exist either . . ." Let us be logical enough to realize the true consequences . . . *But,* with Israel, with Jesus, some of us do believe in God; we are happy to believe, and we are sure that this is our only chance for survival.

Then we can joyfully sing this hymn!

PSALM 117

הַלְלוּ אֶת־יְהוָה כָּל־גּוֹיִם

STRONG IS HIS LOVE FOR US

1 Alleluia!

O praise the Lord, all you nations,
acclaim him all you peoples!

2 Strong is his love for us;
he is faithful for ever.

A FIRST READING: WITH ISRAEL

The structure of this short poem is very clear:

 1. It is a summons extended to men and women through-out the earth to praise and acclaim the Lord.

 2. The reasons for praising are given as a response: strong is his love, eternal his faithfulness.

Let us take advantage of the brevity of this psalm to repeat that parallelism is one of the main devices of Hebrew poetry. Verses echo each other two by two; the same thought is thus expressed twice in balanced, symmetrical phrases. This makes for a "swinging" sound effect, accentuated by the fact that the Jews do sway when they sing these verses, in a sort of peaceful sacred dance:

Praise the Lord	all you nations
Acclaim Him	all you peoples
His *Love*	is strong
His *Faithfulness*	is everlasting

This allows us to understand an important point about biblical theology. We see that two words are placed in parallel: *love* and *faithfulness* (which is sometimes translated by "love" and "truth"). This parallelism shows us that the "truth" of God is not only of the order of intelligence, but of the order of love, of being "true to love." We find these two words together more than a thousand times in the Bible, and they always refer to the theme of the Covenant.

A SECOND READING: WITH JESUS

This short psalm expresses the very essence of our faith.

 1. *Universality* is an essential attitude of Jesus, and the gospel is nothing more than the extension of the Covenant (which had, until then, been reserved for the "Chosen") to all nations, to all men and women. The evangelist summed up Christ's mission when he said that he came and died in order to "gather together in unity the children of God who had been scattered"

(Jn 11:52). This essential formula has been re-introduced into the eucharistic prayer by the Vatican Council.

2. *God's Faithful Love* is one of the main themes of Jesus' thoughts, and the revelation of God as our "Father" follows exactly the ideas of this psalm.

A THIRD READING: WITH OUR TIME

1. *A Psalm for Vacation*—We often go on vacation to broaden the circle of our otherwise narrow relationships; we meet new faces, new cultures, and new nations. Thanks to modern means of transportation, the entire world is practically at our doorstep.

Why could we not, as Christians, also see in this phenomenon a manifestation of God's plan? In his *love* he wants to unite all of his children, he wants them to meet as brothers and sisters—which they already are—even though they do not know it.

Also, everywhere in the world, there are men and women who thirst for prayer and praise. Our vacation trips could be an opportunity to discover and learn to respect different ways of worshipping God.

2. *A Psalm to Broaden Our Minds and Our Hearts*—"Go then and make disciples out of *all* the nations!" This was the scope of the mission which was burning in our Lord's heart. What have we done with it? How narrow are our small cliques, our socio-economic milieux, our national and racial boundaries, seem when we look at them in the light of God's plan!

Praying this psalm also means broadening our horizons and engaging ourselves in the service of the universe.

3. *Strong Is His Love*—God, valiant in battle, is the One who wins victory over all of his enemies. But our God is not a domineering God who crushes people; he is not the father in front of whom all children cringe. He is "all-powerful Love." Jesus gave us the key we need to understand this when he asked us—following God's example—not to "lord it" over people and not to crush our subordinates, but to become the servants of our brothers and sisters. Yes, it is necessary to say it again because Jesus himself told us: God became a servant . . . he became

"love in service" and it is in this capacity that he is the strongest. The only definitive image of God is ultimately that of Jesus on the cross. Yes, his love for us is the strongest!

4. *His Faithfulness Is Everlasting*—O, to be faithful! We are so flighty and inconsistent! We are capable of loving a little, once in a while, and then our love fades.

Faithfulness and perseverance are truly divine qualities, and even when we are unfaithful to God, God remains faithful to us.

We have here one of the most profound elements of the sacrament of marriage: the promise of fidelity, which is at the heart of the sacrament. It is a grace, a gift of God, and it requires a healing of our inconstancy and our weaknesses.

PSALM 118

היחו לַיהוָה הַלְלוּ יָהּ

THIS DAY WAS MADE BY THE LORD

1 Alleluia!

Give thanks to the Lord for he is good,
for his love endures for ever.

* * *

2 Let the sons of Israel say:
"His love endures for ever."
3 Let the sons of Aaron say:
"His love endures for ever."
4 Let those who fear the Lord say:
"His love endures for ever."

5 I called to the Lord in my distress;
he answered and freed me.
6 The Lord is at my side; I do not fear.
What can men do against me?
7 The Lord is at my side as my helper;
I shall look down on my foes.

8 It is better to take refuge in the Lord
than to trust in men:
9 it is better to take refuge in the Lord
than to trust in princes.

10 The nations all encompassed me;
in the Lord's name I crushed them.
11 They compassed me, compassed me about;
in the Lord's name I crushed them.

12   They compassed me about like bees;
      they blazed like a fire among thorns.
      In the Lord's name I crushed them.

13   I was thrust down, thrust down and falling
      but the Lord was my helper.
14   The Lord is my strength and my song;
      he was my saviour.
15   There are shouts for joy and victory
      in the tents of the just.

      The Lord's right hand has triumphed;
16   his right hand raised me.
      The Lord's right hand has triumphed;
17   I shall not die, I shall live
      and recount his deeds.
18   I was punished, I was punished by the Lord,
      but not doomed to die.

19   Open to me gates of holiness:
      I will enter and give thanks.
20   This is the Lord's own gate
      where the just may enter.
      I will thank you for you have answered
      and you are my saviour.

22   The stone which the builders rejected
      has become the corner stone.
23   This is the work of the Lord,
      a marvel in our eyes.
24   This day was made by the Lord:
      we rejoice and are glad.

25   O Lord, grant us salvation;
      O Lord, grant success.
26   Blessed in the name of the Lord
      is he who comes.
      We bless you from the house of the Lord;

27 the Lord God is our light.
    Go forward in procession with branches
    even to the altar.
28 You are my God, I thank you.
    My God, I praise you,
29 Give thanks to the Lord for he is good;
    for his love endures for ever.

■

AN INVITATION TO PRAISE
    Why praise?
    Because of God's LOVE
    **All the members of the crowd, the priests and the faithful
    are invited to praise in alternating voices.**

THE TRAGIC SITUATION
    in which Israel found herself
    **—in their despair they cried out to God and they were
       rescued . . .**
    —they were surrounded by enemy nations . . .
    —but all the forces of evil have been destroyed . . .
    —they are now celebrating the joy of victory . . .
    —It *Is* God who saved us . . .
    —He saved us from *death*.

**THE CELEBRATION, THE SACRIFICE OF THANKSGIVING
IN THE TEMPLE**
    The Levites organize the ceremony . . .
    The King takes part in it in a privileged manner . . .
    The worshippers participate by their acclamations . . .
    Dancing around the altar, they sing and shout:
    —solemn profession of faith of the king . . .
    —and echoed by the congregation . . .

■

A FIRST READING: WITH ISRAEL

This psalm was used for the first time in the year 444 B.C., during the Feast of Booths (Ne 8:13–18) and it is still part of the ritual of this feast. It is a dialogue between the various actors taking part in the celebration: the Levites, the king, and the congregation. We can imagine the festive lyricism, the contagious enthusiasm and the rhythmic joy that burst forth from this song of many voices. The Feast of Booths was the most popular festival. The Court of Women was illuminated throughout the night; a solemn procession would go to the Pool of Siloam to get "living water," and for seven consecutive days, people would live in "tents" made out of branches, in commemoration of the long years of the march of freedom through the desert. In the temple, the worshippers would express their joy by dancing around the altar, with one hand waving a green palm while the other hand was resting on their neighbor's shoulder. They would dance around the altar while swaying from side to side and singing "Alleluia! Blessed is he who comes in the name of the Lord!"

A SECOND READING: WITH JESUS

According to the three synoptic gospels (Mt 212:42; Mk 12:10; Lk 20:17) Jesus explicitly applied this psalm to himself to conclude his parable of the wicked tenants: "The stone which had been rejected by the builders became the cornerstone." Jesus, in this quote, saw himself as the "stone" rejected by the chiefs of the people (a prophetic vision of his death) but which would become the cornerstone in the spiritual building of the people of God.

On Palm Sunday, the same evangelists carefully took note of the fact that the crowd was acclaiming Jesus with the very words of the psalm: "Hosannah! Blessed is he who comes in the name of the Lord!"

Let us not forget that the king we are talking about in this psalm is actually a symbolic king. All exegetes are unanimous in dating this psalm after the exile, at a time when Israel no longer had a king. Who then is this King? This king who crushed all his foes is the *messianic king,* and the victory being celebrated is the *eschatological victory,* the complete and decisive victory of God over all the forces of evil. The *work of God* refers to his salvific work, to the redemption from sin and death. The *day* the Lord has made is of course the "Day of Yahweh" on which his kingship will be truly manifest.

How moving it is, then, to put this psalm on the lips of our Lord: it is *he* who is talking and inviting the whole crowd to take part in his celebration of thanksgiving. He is the king.

Let us reread the psalm in this perspective. And there is nothing artificial in wanting to make this prayer the prayer of Jesus of Nazareth, since we know for a fact that Jesus did sing this psalm before the Passover supper, every year of his life on earth, but especially on Holy Thursday, since this hymn was part of the traditional Hallel.

A THIRD READING: WITH OUR TIME

Easter is indeed the "Day the Lord has made!" It would be vain to search the past in the hope of finding the historical victory or the particular event in the life of Israel for which this prayer of thanks, this *eucharist,* was composed.

The psalmist obviously did not know about Jesus of Nazareth, about his death and resurrection, but he was expecting the messiah, the king, the Anointed, the Christ! When we sing this psalm with Jesus on Easter Day, we celebrate the victory of God over evil. Let us rejoice and be especially thankful for this feast day! It is of his own resurrection that Jesus sang on that evening!

PSALM 121

אֶשָּׂא עֵינַי אֶל־הֶהָרִים

Israel's Guard

1 I lift up my eyes to the mountains:
   from where shall come my help?
2 My help shall come from the Lord
   who made heaven and earth.

3 May he never allow you to stumble!
   Let him sleep not, your guard.
4 No, he sleeps not nor slumbers,
   Israel's guard.

5 The Lord is your guard and your shade;
   at your right side he stands.
6 By day the sun shall not smite you
   nor the moon in the night.

7 The Lord will guard you from evil,
   he will guard your soul.
8 The Lord will guard your going and coming
   both now and for ever.

■

Progressive rhythm: repetitions
—help
—help

  —does not sleep   **guard**
  —does not sleep   **guard**
                         guard

The Lord guards you
The Lord guards your soul
The Lord guards your going and coming ...

■

A FIRST READING: WITH ISRAEL

This is a song of Ascents following a progressive rhythm, which suggests that a second chorus echoes the words of the first chorus.

All of the images are inspired by the theme of the pilgrimage: before leaving on his journey, the traveler explores the horizon to find the proper direction, toward this "mountain of Zion," toward this high place where the temple has been built. Then he sets off, taking care not to twist his foot on the rocky roads. Every night the caravan chooses a watchman to sound the alarm in case of danger. The role of the guard was of prime importance during the perilous journeys of those days: there were bandits and wild beasts. The coolness of the shade was especially valued during the long hours of walking, and the bright rays of the moon had to be softened for these pilgrims who slept under the open sky. Finally, it was not enough to arrive safely; one also had to return home safely—hence the expression "your going and coming."

Clearly, these images reminded the Hebrews of the long march of the Exodus during which a protective cloud would filter out the blazing sun of the desert.

We must take note, once more, of the importance of the local community which encouraged and prayed for the pilgrim. It seems, from the usage of the second-person pronoun, that the first stanza comes from the lips of the pilgrim, while the other stanzas sound like the pledge of support of the pilgrim by those who are staying behind.

A SECOND READING: WITH JESUS

The prevailing feeling of this psalm is confidence in a God who watches over the faithful. This is one of the attitudes Jesus also tried to instill in his listeners: "There is no need to be afraid, little flock, for it has pleased your Father to give you the kingdom" (Lk 12:32). ". . . Every hair on your head has been counted. So there is no need to be afraid" (Mt 10:30). Jesus also asked his father to "guard" his disciples (Jn 17:11).

Our Lord himself experienced this deep sense of security

that surrounds whoever puts his trust in the Father. The psalmist confides to us that God is at the right hand of the faithful, and Jesus echoes this when he tells us: "I am never alone" (Jn 8:16; 16:32).

"The Lord will guard you from evil," the psalmist said, and Jesus presented himself as this vigilant guardian who defends his flock against the aggressor and goes in search of the one lost sheep that is in danger.

This psalm even reminds us of one of the paradoxical passages of the gospel. The faithful stated with assurance that "The Lord sleeps not nor slumbers." Yet, one day, Jesus did fall asleep in the midst of a dangerous storm on the Sea of Galilee. Even then, although Jesus was asleep in his friends' boat, he was truly their safety and he did reproach them with their lack of trust (Mt 8:24). Our true safety lies beyond what is merely human and tangible.

A THIRD READING: WITH OUR TIME

1. *God Never Ceases to Support the Work of His Hands*—"God Never Sleeps!"—Psalm 121 presents to us a vigilant God, an ever-loving God, an ever-working God. God is truly our contemporary. When we state that God is "eternal," we think of a never-ending continuum, going way back into "the past," and extending way ahead into "the future." But this temporal description does not account for eternity. Rather, we should think of eternity as an eternal "present." Because we, as human beings, are immersed in the flow of time, we must live our relationship with God as a "present" relationship, in the present time. At this very moment, you are thinking about me, Lord. At this very moment, you are watching over me. And when we meet in prayer, Lord, at a given moment in time, you are with me . . . The universe is maintained in existence through your continual creation, through your assiduous and untiring love. "He sleeps not nor slumbers, Israel's guard." He has the whole world in his vigilant hand, the entire world, the world of today, now and for ever.

2. *We Are Pilgrims, On the Way*—God is the Supreme Being, living in the fullness of today. We, on the other hand, are

in a continual state of "becoming." We are always "on the way," *in via*. In this sense, pilgrimages or migrations are profound symbols of the human condition. The history of nations and civilizations, as well as of individuals, is but a "long march." Grant us, O Lord, that we may never cease to lift up our eyes toward the goal, that we may never give up hope but always take another step, just one more step, even if our foot does sometimes stumble.

3. *Safety: "The Lord Will Guard Your Going and Coming."* —The word "guard" is used six times in this psalm. Curiously enough, modern society despises safety-seeking and admires risk-taking. Yet members of this same society buy every possible type of insurance. But all these attempts at security, however useful they may be, are for the most part laughable. Never before our time has there been so much mental depression or so many men and women who break down and end up like tempest-tossed wrecks.

Lord, give us this profound safety that only you can give. As the psalm itself suggests, do save our foot from stumbling, be our shade so that the sun will not strike us, guard us from all harm through every moment of your everlasting presence, now and for ever.

4. *None of Us Is Alone On the Road*—In the days of old, when someone decided to go on a pilgrimage, it meant leaving the protected environment of the village community and facing countless dangers on difficult roads. (One could very well end up under the claws of a lion, or the knife of a highway robber.) We understand why the local community would spiritually take charge of the pilgrim, and how the pilgrim would only leave after praying with them and receiving a blessing from them: "May he never allow you to stumble! Let him sleep not, your guard!" During the long, hazardous trip, the community would continue to pray for the one who was on the road.

Help us, Lord, to take care of our brothers and sisters. Help us not to walk by ourselves but in a spirit of solidarity with our fellow human beings.

PSALM 122

PEACE UPON JERUSALEM!

1 I rejoiced when I heard them say:
 "Let us go to God's house."
2 And now our feet are standing
 within your gates, O Jerusalem.

3 Jerusalem is built as a city
 strongly compact.
4 It is there that the tribes go up,
 the tribes of the Lord.

 For Israel's law it is,
 there to praise the Lord's name.
5 There were set the thrones of judgement
 of the house of David.

6 For the peace of Jerusalem pray:
 "Peace be to your homes!
7 May peace reign in your walls,
 in your palaces, peace!"

8 For love of my brethren and friends
 I say: "Peace upon you!"
9 For love of the house of the Lord
 I will ask for your good.

■

JOY

"God's house"

Jerusalem
Jerusalem

217

there
there
there

HAPPINESS   **Jerusalem**
PEACE
PEACE
HAPPINESS

PEACE
"God's house"

■

A FIRST READING: WITH ISRAEL

This is a "Song of Ascents" following a measured rhythm, with a repetition of key words.

After a long trip, the pilgrims are finally in front of Jerusalem. One of them bursts out in cries of joy and admiration. How beautiful is the city! One can imagine the astonishment of the villagers or the nomads when they saw all these buildings in a well-designed pattern: the houses, the streets, the palace and the temple in the middle; everything surrounded with high walls and sturdy towers.

Notice the marvelous literary qualities of this short poem. The tenor of the whole piece is given in the first line—*Joy*—and so is the profound reason for this joy: *"The house of the Lord."* Yes, this is the city where Yahweh dwells. Then the name of the city, lovingly repeated, is surrounded with a garland of phonetic flowers and alliterations which unfortunately can not be translated exactly.

The psalm-writer verbally caresses his beloved city, and the Hebrew word for peace (*shalom*) contains the same consonants as the word for Jerusalem (*Jerushalaim*). When it is sung in Hebrew, this hymn is a small musical jewel composed by a great poet.

There is perfect unity not only in the form but also in the profound significance of the poem: Jerusalem, the capital city toward which everything converges, the city whose architecture underlines its cohesion. The city whose name means "peace" also symbolizes the unity of the scattered tribes . . . and it is the faith in the same God whose glory dwells in the temple which is the cement of this fraternal community.

A SECOND READING: WITH JESUS

It is in that city, unique in all the world, that Jesus died and rose from the dead! It is in that city that the first eucharist was celebrated, this mystery of brothers and sisters gathered around the body of Christ which is the new temple of God.

It is towards that city that Jesus of Nazareth went every year of his earthly life with the crowd of pilgrims and joined in singing this psalm.

It is in that city that every year millions of believers from Judaism and Christianity go to worship the same God . . . although they may remain "separated" or even "enemies." But in this endeavor, in this march towards the same holy place they subconsciously affirm the great dream of humankind: Peace, joy, and love among all races, all peoples as brothers and sisters of the same God.

It is in that city, the true capital of the world, that Jesus gave his life in order to "gather into one the scattered children of God" (Jn 11:52). It is in that city that on Pentecost Day, Jesus founded a community of men and women of every race and tongue—the church—in which the human race finds a place where we can all "be *One, in peace.*"

And now, thanks to the celebration of the eucharist, every city in the world, every place where the mysterious Bread of Life is present is a "house of the Lord."

"I rejoiced when I heard them say: 'Let us go to God's house!' " Do you know, my friends, that this house of God is right at your door, at the end of your street, in your own neighborhood? There is no need to take a long, arduous trip to *Jerushalaim* . . . Just walk into a church and stand in front of the tabernacle and you will be in the City of Peace, in Jerushalaim. Now kneel down and let yourself be overwhelmed by the great peace-joy-happiness which comes from God who loves us so much that he wanted to "plant his tent in our midst," for "The World became flesh and he lived among us." Thank you, Lord!

A THIRD READING: WITH OUR TIME

1. *Universal Yearning for Peace, Joy and Happiness*—We don't have much transposing to do in order to truly pray this psalm in the heart of our present world . . . O Lord, may all humankind become like Jerusalem, "a city strongly compact" to which all the tribes and all the races will converge. May all the peoples also converge towards one another . . . Let there be peace on earth.

2. *Unity—Solidarity*—More than the unity of its architectural structure or than its geographic situation (on top of a mountain) it is a common history and a common destiny that

contributed to the unity of Jerusalem. What constitutes the unity of the human race is also our common destiny. Since we all share the same small planet, we will have to learn how to live together as brothers and sisters—in peace.

3. *Joy*—We are going to the house of the Lord. Pilgrimages have a definite symbolical meaning: to leave one's home, to face the dangers and the fatigue of a long trip, to count the days, to gaze upon a goal so remote at first, but coming closer every day . . . and finally to arrive in view of the holy place one has desired for so long. It is, after all, the parable of the human condition on its journey to the house of God. By the way, are we truly on a journey toward God? Do we see our life as progressing towards a goal, towards *Somebody?*

4. *David—Jesus Christ—Christ the King*—Do you realize that at the time the Jews were praying this psalm (as they still do) the house of David no longer reigned? How then could they possibly say: "There were set the thrones of judgment of the house of David?" This does not make sense unless we inject into these words the waiting and the yearning for the Messiah, the Son of David—according to the promise (2 S 7:1–17). We know that Jesus, the Prince of Peace, did come, and we can pray this psalm and think of the One who came to fulfill the "New Covenant."

PSALM 126   בְּשׁוּב יְהוָה אֶח־שִׁיבַת צִיֹּון

DELIVER US, O LORD, FROM OUR BONDAGE!

1   When the Lord delivered Zion from bondage,
    It is like a dream.
2   Then was our mouth filled with laughter,
    on our lips there were songs.

    The heathens themselves said: "What marvels
    the Lord worked for them!"
3   What marvels the Lord worked for us!
    Indeed we are glad.

4   Bring back, O Lord, our people from captivity
    like torrents in the Negeb.*
5   Those who are sowing in tears
    will sing when they reap.

6   They go out, they go out, full of tears,
    carrying seed for the sowing:
    they come back, they come back, full of song,
    carrying their sheaves.

■

THE GREAT AND WONDROUS DEED OF GOD:
DELIVERANCE FROM BONDAGE
—what was humanly impossible became possible

---

* For v. 4 the Grail version reads:
"Deliver us, O Lord, from our bondage
as streams in dry land."

IS BEING PARTLY FULFILLED:
—by the return from captivity in Babylon . . .

PRAYER FOR TOTAL AND DECISIVE FULFILLMENT:
—two metaphors: water in the desert . . .
the ripening of the seed . . .
—we go from the tears of sowing
to the joy of the harvest . . .

■

A FIRST READING: WITH ISRAEL

This psalm is a "Song of Ascents," part of a collection of psalms which the Jews sang on their way to Jerusalem. The vocabulary ("they go out, they go out . . . they come back, they come back") suggests an immense procession of worshippers advancing towards the temple, perhaps with their hands full of sheaves which they were going to offer to the Lord of the harvest.

The literal meaning of the psalm is the return of the captives following the edict of Cyrus in 538 B.C., after fifty years of exile in Babylon.

The historical event becomes for the psalmist the great symbol of all those desperate situations from which only God can deliver us. The beneficiaries of the deliverance themselves can hardly believe what is happening to them; they think that it is only a dream and they let their joy explode. Even "the heathens themselves said: 'What marvels the Lord worked for them!' "

The poet uses two metaphors to express the idea of life springing up again after death: the springs of living water that make the Negeb bloom in the spring . . . and the sowing of the seeds of wheat which must die in the earth in order to give birth to the joy of the harvest.

Let us again note the eschatological dimension of this psalm: salvation is already started, but not yet fulfilled. The pilgrims who are going to Zion are singing about a quadruple deliverance:

—the "ascent" from Egypt toward the Promised Land,

—the "ascent" from Babylon after their captivity,

—the present "ascent" of the pilgrims toward Zion,

—the eschatological "ascent" of all men and women at the end of time.

The only true liberation is ultimately the Passover and the resurrection.

A SECOND READING: WITH JESUS

Let us reread this psalm with Jesus on Easter morning: our Lord just experienced the resurrection and he can now truly ask his

Father to fulfill his work of salvation by delivering all those who are still held captive by the bondage of death.

Jesus often used the image of the seed as a symbol of death and resurrection (Jn 12:24), and many times he compared the kingdom to the harvest (Mt 9:37, 13:30, 13:39; Mk 4:29; Jn 4:35). When Jesus died, "sowing in tears," he knew that he would "reap in joy"; and this is why he told his friends "You are sad now, but I shall see you again, and your hearts will be full of joy" (Jn 16:22).

A THIRD READING: WITH OUR TIME

1. *A Saving God, A Liberating God*—Do we truly believe that God is the master of the impossible? The Hebrews returning from exile had a hard time believing it; their situation seemed so incredible, so fantastic! What about me? What about that hopeless situation, this seemingly definitive failure, this sin so deeply rooted in my life, or this tragedy that destroyed a life?

Christian hope is not a vague longing that things will eventually work out for the best; it is the certitude that God is performing great deeds for us, that he will save what was lost, that he will truly "bring back the captives." It is the certitude that the Master of the harvest is in the process of bringing his harvest to fruition (Mk 4:26-29).

2. *God Wants Us to Collaborate with Him*—Salvation is a free gift and in this sense we could say that it happens without us, or at least that it is totally beyond our efforts; but this would be forgetting that God created us free and that we are not puppets which God controls from far away. This psalm is actually a program of action and of responsibility: "Those who sow in tears sing as they reap!" In this sense, salvation cannot happen without us! (As Augustine said: "He who redeemed us without any help from us will not save us without our cooperation."

3. *The Positive Role of the Cross*—To collaborate with the work of salvation means that we must be ready to die, that "the seed must die in order to bear fruit," that we must bear our trials in communion with the mystery of the cross of Jesus Christ.

4. *This World Is Only A Beginning*—If you are reading this

psalm for the first time, you will notice that it begins in an atmosphere of exultation; and in the first two stanzas, deliverance seems to have been accomplished forever. Why then are the next two stanzas so full of nostalgia?

No matter how wonderful the return of the exiles might have been, it was only partial and disappointing; and after the songs of praise and the laughter, the painful struggle of humankind went on. We can never say it too often: the promised kingdom of God will achieve its full development only at the resurrection. In the meantime, we must "sow in tears" and wait, comforted by the knowledge that the Parousia (the glorious coming of Christ) is at hand. The seed is germinating—slowly but surely—and the harvest is ripening.

PSALM 128 　　אַשְׁרֵי כָּל־יְרֵא יְהוָה

MAY YOU SEE YOUR CHILDREN'S CHILDREN

1　O blessed are those who fear the Lord
　　and walk in his ways!

2　By the labour of your hands you shall eat.
　　You will be happy and prosper;
3　your wife like a fruitful vine
　　in the heart of your house;
　　your children like shoots of the olive,
　　around your table.

4　Indeed thus shall be blessed
　　the man who fears the Lord.
5　May the Lord bless you from Zion
　　all the days of your life!
6　May you see your children's children
　　in a happy Jerusalem!

　　On Israel, peace!

■

HAPPY ARE THOSE WHO ARE "WITH" GOD
　　—to adore God . . .
　　—to walk in his path . . .

WORK . . .

HUSBAND AND WIFE . . .　　　—the vine

227

CHILDREN . . .   **—the olive tree**

THE CITY AT PEACE . . .
   Long life.

■

A FIRST READING: WITH ISRAEL

This is a "Song of Ascents" sung by the pilgrims as they were going up to Jerusalem. The final formula is a blessing which the priests gave to the pilgrims upon their arrival. "May the Lord bless you from Zion all the days of your life!"

We have here an idyllic picture of family happiness. It is a family where people live in piety and love and are satisfied with their manual labor.

In Israel it was customary to think that men and women who were virtuous were happy and were already receiving their reward on this earth. Because we have been formed by an often disincarnated spirituality, we sometimes think that material goods are to be despised. Biblical thought is much more realistic when it teaches us that God created us for happiness on this earth. So why should we feel guilty when we are happy? Why don't we instead thank God for our happiness and wish the same for everybody?

Let us not fall into the other extreme and reduce everything to a simplistic equation: If you are good, you will be happy, and if you are bad, you will be unhappy! We unfortunately know that righteous people fail and suffer while wicked ones succeed. Suffering is not a punishment but a fact of life, and material success on this earth is not always a proof of virtue.

A SECOND READING: WITH JESUS

"Blessed are those who fear the Lord and walk in his ways!" In the Beatitudes, Jesus repeated: "Blessed . . . blessed . . . blessed . . ." he always promised happiness to all who listen to the word of God and put it into practice.

"Your wife will be like a fruitful vine . . . your children like shoots of the olive." In the Gospel of Mark we read: "What God has united, human beings must not divide" (Mk 10:9).

There are also some mystical allusions in this psalm: Jesus has a spouse, the church (Rv 19:7, 21:2; Mt 9:15, 25:1; Jn 3:29; 2 Co 11:2); we are the children he gathers around his table in the eucharist, and it is "by the labor of (his) hands," the labor of his painful passion that he fed us and gave us happiness.

The vine is also the image of the church, the image of the

loving union between Jesus and the human race: "I am the vine, you are the branches . . . be fruitful . . ." (Jn 15). In the parable of the two sons, the father said: "My boy, go and work in the vineyard . . ." (Mt 21:28).

"You shall see . . . a happy Jerusalem." Jesus shed tears over the city and longed for its happiness (Lk 19:41). And John tells us that heaven will be like a "New Jerusalem coming out of Heaven from God, prepared as a bride dressed for her husband" (Rv 21:2-3).

A THIRD READING: WITH OUR TIME

1. *To Adore God . . . To Walk In His Ways*—Teilhard de Chardin sums up the basic rules of happiness in three verbs: to be, to love, and to adore:

—*To be*—In order to be happy, we must react against the line of least resistance. This is the reason for *work*.

—*To love*—In order to be happy, we must react against egotism. This is the reason for *family*.

—*To adore*—In order to be fully happy we must transfer the focus of our existence to that which is greater than we are. In order to reach joy, we must subordinate our life to a Life that is greater than ours: we must *adore*.

Our ideal, therefore, should be to develop ourselves, then to give ourselves to somebody, and finally to surrender our lives to Somebody who is greater than we are.

2. *Marriage and Conjugal Love*—Divine realities, divine blessings. Human love has been created by God and desired by God. Let us pray this psalm for all those we love, that they may love more and that they may know happiness.

3. *Work and Society*—The happiness of Jerusalem conditions the happiness of every family. No man or woman, no family, can build their happiness at the expense of the happiness of others. The social dimension of our lives is constantly emphasized in the Bible. Let us pray for our city, for our country and for our fellow citizens.

4. *Happiness*—We all have a tendency to turn to God only when things go wrong. Let us rediscover praise and joyful prayer. Let us pray when things go well and let us give thanks!

PSALM 138

אוֹדְךָ בְכָל־לִבִּי

YOUR HAND WILL DO ALL THINGS FOR ME

1 I thank you, Lord, with all my heart,
   you have heard the words of my mouth.
   In the presence of the angels I will bless you.
2 I will adore before your holy temple.

   I thank you for your faithfulness and love
   which excel all we ever knew of you.
3 On the day I called, you answered;
   you increased the strength of my soul.

4 All earth's kings shall thank you
   when they hear the words of your mouth.
5 They shall sing of the Lord's ways:
   "How great is the glory of the Lord!"

6 The Lord is high yet he looks on the lowly
   and the haughty he knows from afar.
7 Though I walk in the midst of affliction
   you give me life and frustrate my foes.

   You stretch out your hand and save me,
   your hand will do all things for me.
   Your love, O Lord, is eternal,
   discard not the work of your hands.

■

I GIVE YOU THANKS
   —because you have heard my prayer . . .
   —because of your faithfulness and love . . .

231

—because of your word . . .
—because you gave me courage . . .

ONE DAY ALL WILL GIVE YOU THANKS
—When they discover this same word . . .
—they will also sing your glory . . .
Lord Almighty
who looks on the lowly
and deflates the haughty.
Lord who gives life
who destroys evil,
who saves.
Lord who is *love* eternal!

"Discard not the work of your hands," *My Love!*

■

A FIRST READING: WITH ISRAEL

This psalm proclaims the *transcendence* of God: "How great is the glory of the Lord!" All authentic religions do this; this is not original . . . but we must nevertheless take the time to let ourselves be overwhelmed by this feeling of *adoration* which makes us bow down—with our faces to the ground—(as the original Hebrew psalm tells us) when we realize in front of *whom* we really stand.

What is more original in the way God reveals himself to Israel is the fact that this transcendent God "looks on the lowly" with love. O the marvel of the infinitely great paying attention to the infinitely small! God's grandeur is not overpowering, it is the grandeur of *love*, it is this *hesed*, this feeling that reaches to the depths of our soul. The word *hesed* is used twice in this psalm. Since God is Love, God *gives love*, *God saves*. God fights against anything that is evil, he "frustrates my foes, (his) hand will do all things for me . . . O Lord, discard not the work of your hands!"

Finally, this message, this *word* which at first is joyfully welcomed by Israel, is eventually *meant for all of humankind.* "All earth's kings shall thank you when they hear the word of your mouth." The kings are the representatives of their people; it is through them that all the nations will give thanks to God on the eschatological Day of the Lord. What an amazing universalist vision!

A SECOND READING: WITH JESUS

1. *The Glory of the Father*—"Hallowed by Thy Name, Thy Kingdom come!"—"Father, glorify your name!" (Jn 12:28).

2. *Giving Thanks*—This was the dominant feeling in Jesus' soul. There was a sort of exultation singing deep in his heart and constantly emerging from his lips: "I bless you Father, Lord of heaven and earth, for hiding these things from the learned and the clever and revealing them to little children" (Mt 11:25). And we know that the climactic moment in the life of Jesus was a celebration of thanksgiving which he told us to reenact in memory of him: "Then he took bread, and when he had given thanks, he broke it and gave it to them, saying, 'This is my body

given for you; do this in remembrance of me.' He did the same with the cup after supper . . .'' (Lk 22:19–20).

3. *The Love of the Lowly, of the Poor*—This divine ''look'' reverses situations, deflating those who are inflated with pride, and increasing the courage of the poor. For Jesus the power of the Almighty was the comforting assurance that not one sparrow falls to the earth without our Father in heaven knowing about it.

A THIRD READING: WITH OUR TIME

1. *Rediscovering Adoration*—The more meaningless and God-less our modern world seems, the more we feel the need to immerse ourselves in what is ''greater than we.'' This can lead us on the way to the ''One-that-is beyond-everything,'' toward God. At times we are forced to recognize that God is after all ''the strongest.'' And the amazing thing is—as the psalmist tells us—that our apparent defeat becomes *awe* and *thanksgiving!* For the power of God, his transcendence is that he loves us with tenderness, with *hesed.* How could I not—joyfully—give in and admit my defeat: I am vanquished and I am happy about it!

2. *Rediscovering Love . . . God's Love for Us . . .*—We think too much about our efforts to love God. We should let our-selves be loved by him! I do not know whether I love you, my Lord, but I am sure of one thing, that *you* love me! And this love, your Love, is eternal . . . even though my love may be fleeting, passing and unfaithful. Once you give something it is for good! Once you promise something, it is forever. We give you thanks for your word. God is the source of love! ''And whoever loves truly knows God,'' scripture tells us.

3. *The Universality of God's Plan*—The fact that Israel, the chosen people, was able—over twenty centuries ago—to con-ceive of a universal religion, of a gigantic ''prayer of thanksgiv-ing'' arising from all the peoples shows us how authentic its religious experience is. How about us believers of *today?* Do we sometimes think that our ''eucharists'' are but a small gathering of a few privileged faithful rather than the immense gathering of all of humankind, of the gigantic prow of the ship sailing toward God? One day, all the kings and all the peoples will celebrate—as we do today—a sacrifice of thanksgiving for the love and the truth of God revealed in Jesus Christ who died and rose for us!

PSALM 145

אֲרוֹמִמְךָ אֱלוֹהַי הַמֶּלֶךְ

YOU GRANT THE DESIRES OF ALL WHO LIVE

1   I will give you glory, O God my King,
    I will bless your name for ever.

2   I will bless you day after day
    and praise your name for ever.
3   The Lord is great, highly to be praised,
    his greatness cannot be measured.

4   Age to age shall proclaim your works,
    shall declare your mighty deeds,
5   shall speak of your splendour and glory,
    tell the tale of your wonderful works.
6   They will speak of your terrible deeds,
    recount your greatness and might.
7   They will recall your abundant goodness;
    age to age shall ring out your justice.

8   The Lord is kind and full of compassion,
    slow to anger, abounding in love.
9   How good is the Lord to all,
    compassionate to all his creatures.

10   All your creatures shall thank you, O Lord,
    and your friends shall repeat their blessing.
11   They shall speak of the glory of your reign
    and declare your might, O God,

12   to make known to men your mighty deeds
    and the glorious splendour of your reign.
13   Yours is an everlasting kingdom;
    your rule lasts from age to age.

The Lord is faithful in all his words
and loving in all his deeds.
14 The Lord supports all who fall
and raises all who are bowed down.

15 The eyes of all the creatures look at you
and you give them their food in due time.
16 You open wide your hand,
grant the desires of all who live.

17 The Lord is just in all his ways
and loving in all his deeds.
18 He is close to all who call him,
who call him from their hearts.

19 He grants the desires of those who fear him,
he hears their cry and he saves them.
20 The Lord protects all who love him;
but the wicked he will utterly destroy.
21 Let me speak the praise of the Lord,
let all mankind bless his holy name
for ever, for ages unending.

■

My God, my King . . .

great . . .

powerful . . .

wonderful, glorious . . .

strong . . .

good . . .
just . . .

kind . . .
compassionate . . .

good . . .
kind . . .

glorious king . . .

eternal . . .

faithful . . .
loving . . .
the help of the weak . . .

the source of life . . .

just . . .
loving . . .
close . . .

protector . . .

savior . . .

■

A FIRST READING: WITH ISRAEL

This is an alphabetical psalm in which each verse starts with a letter of the Hebrew alphabet . . . a sign that one wants to celebrate the Covenant in a complete way—from A to Z. The Jews recite this prayer every morning in response to the exhortation of the beginning: "I will bless you day after day," and Jesus must have said it thousands of times. The vocabulary of this hymn of praise is of intense beauty: "to exalt . . . praise . . . bless . . . proclaim."

The psalmist cannot refrain from praising Yahweh, his king. He is boasting about "his glory, his splendor, his greatness, his might,"—truly royal attributes—but he also sings of his "goodness, justice, compassion, love, faithfulness, closeness" which are rather fatherly qualities. Yes, Yahweh is *king,* but this king puts all his power at the service of love and showers his blessings on humankind. He is not a domineering and far-away potentate, but one who takes an interest in his creation and gives life lavishly.

A SECOND READING: WITH JESUS

The entire gospel shows us how much Jesus was "a man turned towards God." He was the messenger of the Father without any personal power and his sole role was to do the Father's work.

Jesus is the living proof and the embodiment of God's compassion. He is the One who "supports all who fail and raises all who are bowed down."

The food Jesus freely gives to men and women is, of course, the "daily bread" he told us to request from his Father, but it is also this mysterious "Bread of Life" given to us in the eucharist.

We know how often Jesus talked about the kingdom of God, and he showed us this kingdom through his many parables. Yes, he is a king, but his kingdom is not of this world.

A THIRD READING: WITH OUR TIME

1. *Transcendence*—Our modern world, marked by atheistic thought, is tempted to deny any form of transcendence. In this

shrinking perspective, Man and Universe suffice for each other. Yet the most lucid among atheists will confess that the human condition is tragic, and some of them have redefined Man as a being who cannot be fulfilled unless he depends on the *other one.*

In the Judeo-Christian tradition, God is the *other one,* the *all other,* the Transcendent One. God is God! And if God were within our reach, if he were of this world, in the realm of the visible, he would then be reduced to our human level and would therefore be diminished. If we could encompass God and fully comprehend him, he would not be any greater than our small brain, but God is not of the same order as the created. He is beyond us in every way, just as the infinite is beyond the finite.

In the perspective of the Judeo-Christian tradition God is also the *all-near,* the Immanent One, "God-with-us," the God of the Covenant. It is only when we keep these two aspects in mind that we have a balanced picture, the perfect balance only Jesus Christ, the God-Man, can achieve.

2. *To Praise—To Bless—To Give Thanks*—Too often we behave like beggars in front of God and our prayers are limited to asking. Let us reread this psalm and rediscover another form of prayer: *praise.*

There is not one request in the entire psalm—only praise —and the praise vocabulary is remarkably intense and varied: "I will give you glory . . . I will bless your name . . . I will praise you . . . They shall proclaim your mighty deeds . . . speak of your splendor and glory . . . tell of your wonderful works . . . recount your greatness . . . recall your goodness . . . ring out your justice."

Our lives would be transformed if we would adopt this positive style of praise instead of remaining at the level of petition which turns inward toward ourselves in order to put God at our service.

3. *Tell Me How You Pray and I Will Tell You Who You Are*—Although we may say: "Thy will be done" we often mean: "*My* will be done!" With the help of this psalm we can learn to change the way we talk to God, by adopting a language of *love* concentrated on *him* rather than on us.

Tell me if your prayer is one of awe and adoration and I will tell you if you truly love him. Tell me if you are willing to "waste time" with God and I will tell you if you truly love him. Tell me whether you spend all your prayer time talking to him, or if you let him talk to you and I will tell you if you truly love him.

PSALM 146

הַלְלִי נַפְשִׁי אֶת־יְהוָה

HE IS HAPPY WHO IS HELPED BY JACOB'S GOD

1 Alleluia!

   My soul, give praise to the Lord;
2 I will praise the Lord all my days,
   make music to my God while I live.

3 Put no trust in princes,
   in mortal men in whom there is no help.
4 Take their breath, they return to clay
   and their plans that day come to nothing.

5 He is happy who is helped by Jacob's God,
   whose hope is in the Lord his God,
6 who alone made heaven and earth,
   the seas and all they contain.

   It is he who keeps faith for ever,
7 who is just to those who are oppressed.
   It is he who gives bread to the hungry,
   the Lord, who sets prisoners free,

8 the Lord who gives sight to the blind,
   who raises up those who are bowed down,
9 the Lord, who protects the stranger
   and upholds the widow and the orphan.

   It is the Lord who loves the just
   but thwarts the path of the wicked.
10 The Lord will reign for ever,
   Zion's God, from age to age.

   Alleluia!

■

I WILL PRAISE GOD ALL MY LIFE . . .

We cannot count on:
  —**mortal powers . . .**
  —**frail human beings . . .**

We can count on:
            GOD
  —**our Creator . . .**
  —**faithful . . .**
  —**our Savior . . .**
  —**beneficent . . .**
  —**friend of the poor . . .**

May He Reign Forever!

■

A FIRST READING: WITH ISRAEL

This "Psalm of Kingship" is the first psalm of the third *hallel* (Psalms 146–150) recited by Jews in the morning. Each one of these psalms starts and ends with *Hallelu-Yah* which in Hebrew means: "Praise Yahweh." Thus the entire Psalter ends in a burst of praise.

The psalmist sings of the love of God in a sort of joyous carillon (easier to recognize in Hebrew because of the repetitions—nine times—of the same grammatical structure called "hymnic participle"). Note the litany of all the unhappy people God helps: the oppressed, the hungry, the blind, the prisoners, the strangers, the widows, the orphans. The misery of the whole world touches God.

A SECOND READING: WITH JESUS

We have no problem placing this psalm in Jesus' mouth, since one would think it is the gospel we are reading here. Jesus, from his birth to his death, always took the side of the poor, and relied solely on his Father.

Many of Jesus' miracles were the fulfillment of this prayer: the multiplication of the bread for the hungry, the opening of blind eyes, and the releasing of those who were prisoners of their sins. At the messianic banquet, it is the poor and the oppressed, the blind and the crippled who will be the guests of honor.

The "beatitudes" we have here are similar to the ones uttered by Jesus: "Happy are those who rely on God . . . happy are those who listen to the Word of God." To these beatitudes correspond maledictions: "He thwarts the path of the wicked" is echoed by "Alas for you who are rich: you are having your consolation now" (Lk 6:24). Jesus often repeated—along the lines of this psalm—that a materialistic life leads to naught. Do you remember the rich farmer who wanted to enlarge his barn? "Put no trust in mortal men . . . they return to clay and their plans come to nothing."

A THIRD READING: WITH OUR TIME

1. *"My Soul, Give Praise to the Lord! I Will Praise the Lord all My Days"*—Do we truly know how to praise? Do we know how to give thanks for the wonders of God's love?

2. *"Put No Trust in Princes in Whom There Is No Help!"*— How can we rely on human beings made out of clay, on the "children of dust" who will one day return to dust? There is no pessimism in this attitude, only the plain and obvious truth! Only God can *save* us. "Only in him is there salvation; for of all the names in the world given to men, this is the only one by which we can be saved" (Ac 4:12).

3. *"He Is Happy Who Is Helped By Jacob's God"*—O Lord, give us this profound happiness. Help us to believe that it is in you and in you only that we can find happiness—the kind of happiness which nothing can tarnish or undermine.

4. *"He Who Alone Made Heaven and Earth, the Seas and All They Contain."*—We must, from time to time, close our eyes and look at God's creation with our mind's eyes. On a cloudless night please gaze at the stars and try to imagine the galaxies . . . think of all the life that swarms on the surface of the earth and at the bottom of the oceans!

5. *"He Who Keeps Faith Forever."*—Immediately after recalling the creative power of God, the psalmist recalls the loving and eternal faithfulness of God as if the two were connected. One could conclude that this great God of the universe is far away, and this is what many philosophers thought. But please listen to this psalm: He takes loving care of the poor and the lowly, the unloved, the unhappy and it is for them that he saves his blessings, while the mighty and the haughty are the object of his curses.

6. *God Sides with the Poor*—What about us? To protect and to help, to care and support: those are divine functions which God entrusted to us. Yes, in spite of the fact that we are but "specks of dust" we possess this amazing dignity which allows us to imitate God. Jesus told us: "Be perfect as the Father is perfect."

PSALM 148

הַלְלוּ אֶת־יְהוָה

PRAISE THE LORD FROM THE HEAVENS!
PRAISE THE LORD FROM THE EARTH!

1 Alleluia!

Praise the Lord from the heavens,
praise him in the heights.
2 Praise him, all his angels,
praise him, all his host.

3 Praise him, sun and moon,
praise him, shining stars.
4 Praise him, highest heavens
and the waters above the heavens.

5 Let them praise the name of the Lord.
He commanded: they were made.
6 He fixed them for ever,
gave a law which should not pass away.

7 Praise the Lord from the earth,
sea creatures and all the oceans,
8 fire and hail, snow and mist,
stormy winds that obey his word;

9 all mountains and hills,
all fruit trees and cedars,
10 beasts, wild and tame,
reptiles and birds on the wing;

11 all earth's kings and peoples,
earth's princes and rulers;
12 young men and maidens,
old men together with children.

13 Let them praise the name of the Lord
    for he alone is exalted.
    The splendour of his name
    reaches beyond heaven and earth.

14 He exalts the strength of his people.
    He is the praise of all his saints,
    of the sons of Israel,
    of the people to whom he comes close.

    Alleluia!

■

A COSMIC HYMN

Up there in the heights of the cosmos ...
    the angels,
    the hosts,
    the sun,
    the moon,
    the stars,
    the heavens.

Down here on planet earth ...
    all the oceans,
    fire, snow and mist,
    winds,
    mountains and hills,
    fruit trees and cedars,
    tame flocks and wild beasts,
    reptiles and birds,

HUMAN BEINGS ... of all conditions,
                   of all races,
                   of all ages,

but especially,
THE FAITHFUL . . .
> **who are a part of his people,**
> **and who "Know" of his "closeness."**

■

A FIRST READING: WITH ISRAEL

This is an invitation to *praise*. The words "praise" or "sing" are repeated twelve times—including the two alleluias at the beginning and the end (since *hallelu-yah* in Hebrew means "Praise God").

This is a *universal* invitation to praise, and the word "all" is repeated seven times. The *whole creation* is invited. Notice the same progression as in the Book of Genesis: first inanimate matter, then animate creatures, and finally human beings, and in particular Israel, the chosen people.

In semitic thought the "sea creatures and all the oceans" represent the *powers of hell* (dragons and lower abysses). Even natural disasters like fire, hail and storm, which are dangerous forces not yet harnessed by man, are also invited to take part in praise. Once more we have here the foretelling of the eschatological triumph of God, the definitive victory of God over all evil forces.

A SECOND READING: WITH JESUS

As previously mentioned, we know for a fact that Jesus did sing this psalm, which is part of the *hallel* recited during the Passover meal. The deepest recesses of Jesus' soul are revealed here. This people whose "strength God exalts," this priestly people entrusted with the praising of God, this people "to whom he comes close," this faithful people was, of course, Israel. We also know that Christ himself was the incarnation of the chosen people.

Following an ancient tradition the last three psalms are sung at the end of Sunday Lauds (and the word "Lauds" comes from the latin *laudare* which means "to praise"). The eucharistic gathering of Christians on Sundays should have this dimension of universal praise; the faithful are the people who—with Jesus Christ—sing praise to God "in the name of all."

A THIRD READING: WITH OUR TIME

1. *Praising God with the Whole Creation*—This is a psalm for summer, a psalm for vacation. We must learn how to see, how

to open our eyes to the marvels of the universe: the mountains and the forests, the animals, the flowers and the stars, men and women, young and old.

2. *Beauty*—Let us be overwhelmed by the greatness and the infinite beauty of God! Let us be overwhelmed by the almost infinite beauty of things. Notice that this psalm does not praise an *abstract God* and does not praise God for his atemporal attributes, but for his creation and for the unfolding of his marvelous deeds throughout human history. There is a kind of narrow pantheism which consists in adoring the universe as if it were a god. As we know, God is even greater and more beautiful than what he created. But let us not forget that the universe is after all "a part of God."

Saint Francis, the Little Poor Man of Assisi, who was detached from any earthly possessions was the balladeer of creation and his "Canticle of Brother Sun" was his way of retelling Psalm 148:

1   Most High, all-powerful, good Lord,
     Yours are the praises, the glory, the honor, and all blessing.
2   To You alone, Most High, do they belong,
     and no man is worthy to mention Your name.
3   Praised be You, my Lord, with all your creatures,
     especially Sir Brother Sun,
     Who is the day and through whom You give us light.
4   And he is beautiful and radiant with great splendor;
     and bears a likeness of You, Most High One.
5   Praised be You, my Lord, through Sister Moon and the
         stars,
     in heaven You formed them clear and precious and beautiful.
6   Praised be You, my Lord, through Brother Wind,
     and through the air, cloudy and serene, and every kind of
         weather
     through which You give sustenance to Your creatures.
7   Praised be You, my Lord, through Sister Water,
     which is very useful and humble and precious and chaste.
8   Praised be You, my Lord, through Brother Fire,
     through whom You light the night

and he is beautiful and playful and robust and strong.

9   Praised be You, my Lord, through our Sister Mother Earth,
who sustains and governs us,
and who produces varied fruits with colored flowers and
herbs.

10   Praised be You, my Lord, through those who give pardon
for Your love
and bear infirmity and tribulation.

11   Blessed are those who endure in peace
for by You, Most High, they shall be crowned.

12   Praised be You, my Lord, through our Sister Bodily Death,
from whom no living man can escape.

13   Woe to those who die in mortal sin.
Blessed are those whom death will find in Your most holy
will,
for the second death shall do them no harm.

14   Praise and bless my Lord and give Him thanks
and serve Him with great humility.*

Closer to our time, Teilhard de Chardin also rewrote Psalm
148 in his "Hymn to Matter":

Blessed be you, rough matter, sterile glebe, harsh
rock . . . violent sea . . . irresistible evolution . . . triple
abyss of stars, atoms and generations . . . I bless you,
mortal matter . . . Hand of God, Flesh of Christ, divine
"Milieu" charged with creative power, Ocean stirred
by the Spirit, Clay moulded and breathed into life by
the incarnate Word . . .

---

* From *Francis and Clare: Complete Works,* edited by Regis Armstrong,
O.F.M. Cap. and Ignatius C. Brady, O.F.M. Reprinted by permission of Paulist
Press.

PSALM 149   שִׁירוּ לַיהוָה שִׁיר חָדָשׁ

SING HIS PRAISE IN THE ASSEMBLY OF THE FAITHFUL

1 Alleluia!

Sing a new song to the Lord,
his praise in the assembly of the faithful.
2 Let Israel rejoice in its Maker,
Let Zion's sons exult in their king.
3 Let them praise his name with dancing
and make music with timbrel and harp.

4 For the Lord takes delight in his people.
He crowns the poor with salvation.
5 Let the faithful rejoice in their glory,
shout for joy and take their rest.
6 Let the praise of God be on their lips
and a two-edged sword in their hand,

7 to deal out vengeance to the nations
and punishment on all the peoples;
8 to bind their kings in chains
and their nobles in fetters of iron;
9 to carry out the sentence pre-ordained:
this honour is for all his faithful.

Alleluia!

■

AN INVITATION TO PRAISING GOD
sing!
praise!

251

celebrate!
rejoice!
dance!
play on timbrels and harps!

**FOR GOD LOVES HIS PEOPLE AND GIVES VICTORY
TO THE POOR**
exult!
shout for joy!
praise!
brandish the sword!

**THROUGHOUT HISTORY AND UNTIL THE DAY
OF JUDGEMENT**
the mighty will be vanquished
and judged as pre-ordained,
for the joy of the faithful . . .

■

A FIRST READING: WITH ISRAEL

Psalm 148 praised God for his creation. Psalm 149 praises God throughout history and up to Judgment Day. It is the celebration of the victory of the *hasidim* (the faithful) who are also identified with the *anawim* (the lowly). For this celebration, the entire population welcomes the victorious warriors with patriotic songs and dances, parades with drums and timbrels, swords brandished in the air. According to the ancient tradition the vanquished kings and generals in chains follow the procession of the victors.

For Israel the victory of the "lowly" is also the victory of God, the eschatological victory. The violence and the revenge expressed in the last stanza must be applied to the *evil* which one day will be vanquished on the Day of the Lord. This will be the fulfillment of the kingdom and Zion will truly "exult in her king." Our earthly liturgies are a preview of the celestial liturgy which will celebrate the complete victory of God over all his foes: sin and wickedness, egotism and injustice, suffering and death.

The participation of God's faithful in the royal triumph at the end of time, as well as the association of the "mighty" and the "arrogant" with forces of evil are traditional ideas. Daniel even compared them to malevolent beasts: "The four great beasts are four kings who will rise up from the earth. Those who receive royal power are the holy ones of the Most High" (Dn 7:17).

A SECOND READING: WITH JESUS

When we pray this psalm we concur with the gospel view of the poor: "Blessed are the poor, the Kingdom of Heaven is theirs." And we can already hear in this psalm the Magnificat of Mary: "He has pulled down princes from their thrones and raised high the lowly" (Lk 1:52).

The victory in question is first and foremost the triumph of God over death through the resurrection of Jesus in which we will one day participate.

Paul applied this psalm to the poor of the port of Corinth

among whom "not many are wise by human standards, not many influential, not many from noble families" (1 Co 1:26). He wrote to those *anawim:* "Do you not realize that the holy people of God are to be the judges of the world?" (1 Co 6:2).

It would be erroneous to understand these words as an invitation for the "lowly" to take revenge on the "mighty." At the same time, however, let us not water down those words, but remember that throughout the Bible God constantly sides with the poor and the humble.

A THIRD READING: WITH OUR TIME

1. *Progress*—Our modern world has become very sensitized to the historic dimension of events. While ancient thought conceived of time as a never-ending circle, biblical thought introduced the concept of history and progress. Historical events are not simple and superficial phenomena occurring on a fixed and immobile background. God intervenes in the history of humankind and history proceeds toward a goal. Creation is not something that happened in the past; God is still creating today! Redemption is not something that happened in the past; God is still redeeming us today.

2. *An Invitation To Joy and Praise*—"Let us praise his name with dancing!" Dancing has always played a role in the traditional liturgy of some Eastern countries as an expression of joy in front of God. So, do not be shocked if today some Christians are trying to recapture this tradition, and if they want to accompany their songs with "timbrel and harp" or "guitars and drums." The Psalms have always invited us to do so, urging us to praise God "with dancing and make music with timbrel and harp." If our celebrations are not warmer and more joyful, we run the grave risk of giving a wrong impression of our God. Our God is not a sad God or a defeated God! So let us joyfully celebrate! "Let Israel rejoice in its Maker, let Zion's children exult in their king!"

3. *The Poor Are the Privileged Object of God's Love*—God promised his victory to the poor, the downtrodden, to all those without any human support, to those who, having nothing to expect from this earth, turn their hope toward God and enter into a loving relationship with Him. Love is the key word of the

Covenant. The downtrodden will not always be downtrodden, the lonely will not always be lonely, the sick and the handicapped will not always be tormented in their flesh. The dead will not always be dead: They will come back to life! Let us sing *Alleluia* in anticipation of this victory!

PSALM 150 הַלְלוּ-אֵל

LET EVERY LIVING BEING SING HIS PRAISE

1 ALLELUIA!

Praise God in his holy place,
praise him in his mighty heavens.
2 Praise him for his powerful deeds,
praise his surpassing greatness.

3 O praise him with sound of trumpet,
praise him with lute and harp.
4 Praise him with timbrel and dance,
praise him with strings and pipes.

5 O praise him with resounding cymbals,
praise him with clashing of cymbals.
6 Let everything that lives and that breathes
give praise to the Lord. ALLELUIA!

■

PRAISE, UNIVERSAL ALLELUIA

a universal invitation:—in the temple,
—in heaven.

to praise God:—for his powerful deeds,
—for his majestic being.

—with trumpets, sounded by the priests,
—with lutes and harps, plucked by the levites,

—with strings and pipes, played by all
—with tambourines and dances, used by the women
—with cymbals clanged by all.

Let Everything That Breathes Praise the Lord!

A FIRST READING: WITH ISRAEL

In Hebrew the title of the Book of Psalms is *Praises*. Psalm 150 is the last of the Praises and the conclusion of the book. The symphony ends with ten verses which all start with *Allelu-yah* (*Praise Yahweh!*) We have the decalogue, the ten laws, and here we have ten declarations of praise.

This song of praise is bursting forth in every direction and toward every horizon. God's final victory becomes this eternal *Alleluia* which is echoed back and forth without end. Nothing is left out of the celebration:

All of the cosmos is invited: the holy place which is our human earth, as well as the inviolate heavenly vault, where his divine power is manifest, are all part of this great hymn of praise.

All of humankind: sounding the trumpet was the prerogative of the priests; the lute and the harp were the instruments used in the sanctuary by the cantors/levites; the tambourines are always mentioned in the Bible as being suited to the rhythmic dancing of young girls and women. Finally, everybody was allowed to play strings and pipes, and the cymbals were typical of the *terouah,* a war-cry and a royal acclamation.

All of the musical instruments known at that time! The entire orchestra!

Finally, *all living beings,* not only men and women, but everything that breathes! Even animals are singing God's praises. The Hebrew formula is very powerful: "Let everything that breathes praise the Lord!" This tells us that we should use all our breathing power for this celebration, our entire lung capacity to sound our trumpets, and that we should dance for God until we run out of breath. Let us not forget that in Hebrew thought, the "breath" is the sign of life and comes from God. This last page of the Book of Psalms takes us back to the first page of Genesis which saw the blossoming of *all living things,* of everything that breathes, under the divine breath.

A SECOND READING: WITH JESUS

"I bless you, Father." One day this prayer emerged from the joy-filled soul of Jesus. "Filled with joy by the Holy Spirit, Jesus said: 'I bless you, Father!' '' (Lk 10:21). This must have been the usual atmosphere of his prayer, and the long nights spent with his Father must have resounded with joy and praise: Jesus, more than any other human being knew the powerful deeds of God, which entail creation, redemption, universal salvation, and the final victory over sin and death. Jesus epitomized in his own being all of humankind throughout history.

May we always remember that the Greek word *eucharistia* means "thanksgiving" and "praising." Each one of our eucharists should be our participation in this symphony. Do we come to mass to praise and to sing, or do we only ask and remain silent?

"Then, he took the bread, and when he had given thanks, Jesus broke it and said: this is my body given for you."

We can assume that at the end of the Passover supper, Jesus sang this very psalm which was part of the hallel. Let us imagine Jesus singing these words: His voice must have been warm, melodious, beautiful, vibrant, in rhythm, and well in tune with the apostles who were singing with him.

Let us dream that we could go back to that evening in the Upper Room. We could then listen to a blending of these voices with all of the instruments mentioned before.

But this is not a dream! We are, after all, the "Body of Christ," and every time we sing this psalm, Jesus IS singing with us, and through our voices. This is why we must sing it with all our hearts. And since we are dreaming, let us dream a little longer. Let us dream of heaven as music—magnificent music made for God—with Jesus Christ as choirmaster, conductor, and leader of all the praises!

A THIRD READING: WITH OUR TIME

1. *Joyous Or Sad Religion*—Why is it that some people accuse Christians of being wet blankets? It would be childish to deny the serious questions raised by our human condition: the sufferings of innocent people, misfortune and injustice aggravated by selfishness, petty grudges and jealousies. Nevertheless, God created us for *joy!* This is one of the challenges we Christians face: to proclaim that joy, to believe in that joy in spite of all that

assails us in the world, and to celebrate that joy in our liturgies. Let us not forget that the word "gospel" means "good news." Every liturgy which gathers Christians together should be a foretaste of heaven where "there will be no more death, and no more mourning or sadness or pain" (Rv 21:4), and where our sole occupation will be to praise God with singing, dancing, and music, in an everlasting festival (Rv 4:8–71; 5:8; 14:2; 15:2; 19:1–8).

2. *Music*—Music has always been one of humankind's most important traits, in every century and in every civilization. Nature has always been singing, through the myriads of different sounds which emanate from the wind, the forests, and the springs. This psalm tells us with so much insight something which has been confirmed by science: music is, for the most part, produced by breathing beings. The roar of a wild beast or the song of a bird, as well as the human voice, are actually created by the breath which is exhaled from the lungs and makes the vocal chords vibrate. Music is truly the *sign* of life, the sign of anything that lives, of anything that breathes. We can see why music has always been used for worship and religious ceremonies in every age and every culture. "Whoever sings prays twice," the old adage tells us. When we sing, we tell God with our physical being: "See, Lord, I am alive. You created me for life and for joy. Thank You, Lord!"

But speaking and singing were not enough. Human beings also created all kinds of musical instruments: wind instruments, string instruments, percussion instruments. If all of the instruments invented throughout the ages could be assembled in one museum, there would be millions of flutes and violins; rebecs, harps, lutes and zithers; guitars, mandolins, guzlas; mandoras and balalaikas, cymbalums and tympanums, psalteries, horns, trumpets and bugles; saxhorns and saxophones, Jew's harps, fifes and flageolets, clarinets and oboes, bagpipes, whistles and kazoos, pianos and harpsichords; organs and harmoniums, harmonicas and accordions, record-players and stereos; balafons and coras, drums and tom-toms, xylophones and castanets.

Let the music begin! Praise God! Praise him! Praise him! Alleluia. God is good! God loves us!